BOLIVIAN INDIAN TEXTILES
Traditional Designs and Costumes

104 Illustrations, Including 55 in Full Color

Text & Photography by
Tamara E. Wasserman
&
Jonathan S. Hill

Dover Publications, Inc.
New York

To the nameless weavers of Bolivia,
who have expressed their dreams and traditions
with imagination, artistry and beauty.

The fabrics of a people unlock their social history. They speak a language which is silent, but yet more eloquent than the written page. As memorials of former times, they commune directly with the beholder, opening the unwritten history of the period they represent, and clothing it with perpetual freshness.

— Lewis Henry Morgan, *League of the Ho-dé-no-sau-nee, or Iroquois,* 1851

Published in Canada by General Publishing Company, Ltd., 30 Lesmill Road, Don Mills, Toronto, Ontario.
Published in the United Kingdom by Constable and Company, Ltd., 10 Orange Street, London WC2H 7EG.

Bolivian Indian Textiles: Traditional Designs and Costumes is a new work, first published by Dover Publications, Inc., in 1981.

DOVER *Pictorial Archive* SERIES

Bolivian Indian Textiles: Traditional Designs and Costumes belongs to the Dover Pictorial Archive Series. Up to ten illustrations from this book may be reproduced on any one project or in any single publication, free and without special permission. Wherever possible, include a credit line indicating the title of the book, author and publisher. Please address the publisher for permission to make more extensive use of illustrations in this book than that authorized above.
The republication of this book in whole is prohibited.
Readers wishing to obtain photographic prints of items illustrated herein may write directly to the authors (address given in Foreword; see facing page).

Book design by Carol Belanger Grafton

International Standard Book Number: 0-486-24118-1
Library of Congress Catalog Card Number: 80-69567

Manufactured in the United States of America
Dover Publications, Inc.
180 Varick Street
New York, N.Y. 10014

Foreword and Acknowledgments

The traditional textiles of Bolivia pictured here are among the last remaining examples of a highly perfected weaving art whose roots and inspiration can be traced back to Inca and other pre-Columbian prototypes. The continuity of this rural esthetic culture in the Andes is now being undermined by the effects of economic and social modernization. The ancient values and crafts are being threatened, and are deteriorating or disappearing. Weaving has been one of the most important of these daily activities in Bolivian highland culture for thousands of years, serving utilitarian, social and ceremonial functions for the indigenous Indians. In recent decades, the study and collecting of textiles and costumes have become major fields of interest for students of archaeology, ethnology, art and history, as well as a stimulus for contemporary artists and craftspeople.

With this in mind, the authors have attempted to illustrate, assess and highlight a broad selection of fine textiles from several of the major weaving centers in the Bolivian highlands, and to view the Quechua and Aymará peoples who created them. Although an awareness of exquisite handweaving has existed in South America for over five hundred years, surprisingly little serious research or documentation was done in Bolivia before the 1970s. It is our expectation that the colorful array of textiles presented here will provide weavers, designers, prospective collectors and future researchers with a basic introduction to the consummate artistry of a tradition that is just beginning to receive its due recognition. In this way, we hope to share our own enthusiasm and admiration for Bolivian weaving, and to encourage a more expanded consideration and appreciation of its beauty.

The textiles surveyed here were primarily obtained in the field during several journeys to Bolivia in 1976 and 1977. Unless otherwise noted, all weavings illustrated are from the collection of Jonathan S. Hill. They have appeared in the exhibition "Traditional Bolivian Textiles," circulated throughout the U.S. under the auspices of the Western Association of Art Museums from 1979 to 1981.

The pictures of people and landscapes taken in Bolivia are by Mr. Hill, while the photographs of the textiles are the joint work of the authors.

Any inquiries or comments regarding research, collecting or lecturing about Bolivian weavings are welcomed. Please address such correspondence directly to:

JONATHAN HILL AND TAMARA WASSERMAN HILL
P.O. Box 40616
San Francisco, Calif. 94140

No book is an individual effort. We would like to express our thanks to all those who have helped and guided us in the preparation of this work, which began in 1976. Steve and Gail Berger provided inspiration for our travels and textile collecting in South America. Others who have also shared time and information include Bruce Takami, Laurie Adelson, Roger Yorke and Arthur Tracht. Bob Koch and the Bergers kindly allowed pieces from their collections to be photographed, adding to the historical picture.

Production assistance came from Dennis Geaney, Kate Kline May, Gary Lichtenstein and Michael Rachoff of Acu-Lab, San Francisco. We are grateful to Mary Moser and Jan Janeiro, and to Adele Cahlander's work, for advice on the technical descriptions. Frank Elliott contributed the design and calligraphy for the map of Bolivia.

T. W. H. & J. S. H.

San Francisco, 1978/1980

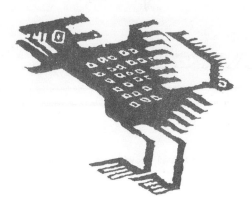

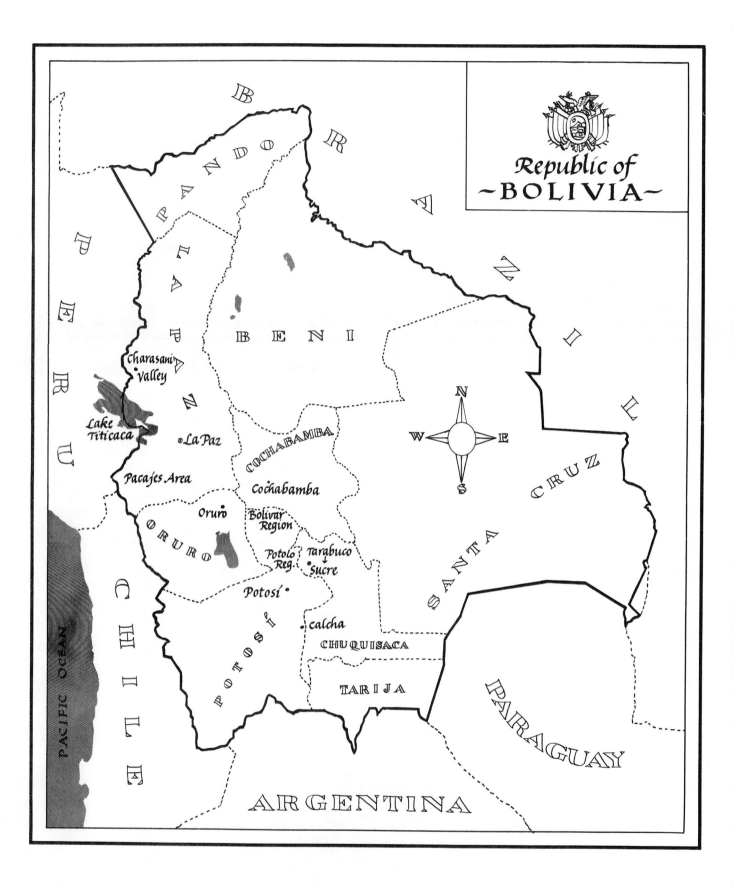

Illus. 1: Map of Bolivia, showing major weaving centers.

Introduction

THE ORIGINS OF WEAVING IN PERU AND BOLIVIA

The origin of man in South America is controversial. It is generally accepted, however, that the ancestors of today's Andean Indians migrated across the Bering Strait from northern Asia approximately 20,000 years ago.[1] They evolved from a nomadic life of hunting and gathering into a pattern of small agrarian settlements. Before fashioning pottery, these settlers made twined cotton fabrics and fish nets, as early as 3000–1200 B.C. in Peru. The use of cameloid fibers began between circa 1400 and 400 B.C.[2] Long before the Christian era, primitive looms were devised, and weaving had reached a masterly degree of sophistication at Paracas, on the Peruvian coast.

During the ensuing centuries, numerous civilizations and phases of material culture succeeded each other along the coast and in the Andean highlands. The major site of ancient culture and religion in Bolivia seems to have been Tiahuanaco, south of Lake Titicaca. From this center a distinctive architectural and artistic style was disseminated throughout the Andes, from approximately 600 to 1100 A.D. Unfortunately, the moist climate at Tiahuanaco (elevation approximately 12,000 feet) has destroyed most of the textiles that may have been buried there. The site's impressively carved stone work is nearly all that remains of a great culture. Most examples of "Tiahuanaco style" tapestry-weave tunics have been discovered in excavations on the arid south coast of Peru; yet it is quite probable that weaving of this type was done in Bolivian territory at a similarly early date as well.

THE INCA EMPIRE AND THE AYMARÁ AND QUECHUA PEOPLES OF THE BOLIVIAN HIGHLANDS

There is a gap in the archaeological records between the decline of the Tiahuanaco culture and the rise of the Incas, the last great Indian empire to emerge in South America. When the Incas entered the territory south of Lake Titicaca about 1450, they encountered various tribes of Indians—the Colla, Lupaca, Canchi, Canas, Pacasas—loosely organized under feuding hereditary rulers, speaking Aymará and other different dialects.

Their descendents in Bolivia have long been known collectively as "Aymarás." By exploiting internal dissensions, the Incas were finally able to conquer these peoples, imposing political and economic changes upon them; however, many refused to accept both Inca customs and the official language, Quechua.

Large numbers of Inca administrators and colonists used the Quechua tongue in what is now Bolivia. Whereas Aymará had once been the prevalent language, subsequent movements of Indian laborers during the Spanish colonial silver-mining eras of the seventeenth and eighteenth centuries accounted for the later predominance of Quechua. In the Bolívar Region and in the Charasani Valley, for example, it appears that Aymará was originally spoken whereas Quechua now prevails. Thus, "Aymará" and "Quechua" represent similar but distinct racial, linguistic and cultural groups. They have retained many of their differences in speech, dress, agricultural methods and traditions over the centuries.[3] Currently in Bolivia, the Aymarás mainly inhabit the arid *altiplano* (plateau, S.)* near Lake Titicaca, but many are steadily moving closer to the city of La Paz, where they are submitting to modernizing influences. In general, Quechuas are found in the mountain valleys of the Cordillera Real range (east and southeast of Lake Titicaca), but other Quechua communities exist in south central Bolivia around the areas of Cochabamba, Potosí and Sucre. They are undoubtedly the lineage of those who were resettled by both the Incas and the Spanish colonizers.[4]

Weaving During and After the Inca Period

Out of the great variety of inventive techniques developed by early weavers, some methods are still being used by contemporary Bolivian Indians. Although each ancient culture developed its own characteristic textile designs and costume styles, we are most familiar with the customs related to Inca usage of cloth, as these were observed and documented by literate Spaniards after their arrival in the New World (Illus. 2). Further

---

*Throughout this Introduction, the letters S., Q. and A. indicate that a foreign term is of Spanish, Quechua or Aymará origin, respectively. "Q./S." indicates a Quechua word in a Spanish adaptation.

PRIMERA CALLE
AVACOGVARMI

se edad de treynta y tres años

muger de ributo
Pa

Illus. 2: Drawing of an Inca woman weaving, from an early 17th-century Peruvian codex by Felipe Guamán Poma de Ayala now in the Kongelige Bibliotek, Copenhagen.

evidence of fine textiles from both Inca and preceding civilizations comes out of excavated graves in the deserts near the Peruvian coast.

The uses of cloth in Inca times were closely associated with the theocratic religion, whose focus was the Inca monarch, a divine personification of the Sun. The basis of Inca mythology may have been linked to earlier highland solar worship, as seen in the "Gateway of the Sun" at Tiahuanaco.[5] A variety of local animistic beliefs were incorporated with veneration for a creator-god, Viracocha, and were associated with agricultural cycles and rituals administered by village medicine men.[6] The solar symbol itself, *inti* (Q.), persists as a stylized diamond-shaped motif in Bolivian weaving from many areas (Plate 17, bottom, and Fig. 1).*

Cloth served a multiplicity of purposes in Inca society. From the most basic need to clothe the body in a cold and mountainous climate, to the expression of personal status and prestige, woven fabrics were of functional and psychological importance. In all kinds of ceremonies,

*"Plates" refer to the color pages, "figures" to the black-and-white section of textile motifs, and "illustrations" to the pictures accompanying this Introduction.

whether celebrating birth, puberty initiations, marriage, the agricultural cycle or death, textiles were offered, worn, exchanged and burned in sacrifice by nobles and peasants alike. Frequently, special new garments were woven for use in the afterlife. The bereaved family also wore garments designated for mourning. A woman's spindle was interred with her, as a remembrance of her most typical daily activity. Some of these practices relating to "rites of passage" continue to be observed in regions of Bolivia such as Charasani, Potolo and Tarabuco.

Early Costume Prototypes

Inca clothing provides us with prototypes for traditional Bolivian costume. The main garment worn by men in Inca times was an untailored, shirt-like tunic called the *unku* (Q.). It was woven in two panels, with the center seam left partially open for the head. The outside edges were sewn together, except for the armholes. A small pouch, the *chuspa* (Q.), served instead of pockets. Finely crafted pieces fitting this description have been found in Bolivia, although they ceased to be made by the 20th century. The Quechua word *unku* is now used to describe the small *ponchito* (S.) that is worn like a yoke or apron as part of the Tarabucan Indians' costume (Illus. 3). It has been suggested that the larger, open-sided *poncho* (S.) was a later development, originating in Chile among the

Illus. 3: A Tarabucan man wearing a modern *unku, chuspas, montera* and leather belt.

Araucanian Indians in the 17th century,[7] and subsequently popularized by the Spanish cavalry.

Inca women wore a tunic-style dress then called an *aksu* (Q.), a cloak-like mantle (*lliclla*, Q.) and a headcloth (*p'anta*, Q.).[8] Garments still referred to by these names continue to form most Quechua women's costumes. Under the Incas, everyone wore some type of distinguishing headgear. One such item was the *llautu* (Q.), a varicolored "belt" that was wrapped around the head or folded in quarters, perhaps like a turban.[9] A modern interpretation of this may be seen in the *wincha* (Q.) of the Charasani Valley (Plate 4, top).

THE SPANISH CONQUEST AND ITS EFFECTS ON INDIAN CULTURE

In 1532, Francisco Pizarro and a small group of Spanish conquistadores overthrew the Inca ruler and began their conquest of his vast empire. Drastic policies were soon put into effect to achieve the main goals of colonization: exploitation of South America's great mineral wealth and conversion of its inhabitants to Christianity. The *mita* (Q.) system of conscripted labor recruited every able Indian man to work periodically in the newly discovered silver mines, forcing them to move from their own localities to distant regions, and thus eroding community structures. Ownership of land was denied the Indians, and exorbitant taxes were exacted by the foreign overlords. Inca religion was discouraged through the destruction of temples and the prohibition of ancient ceremonies.

To meet their tribute obligations, many native villages had begun communal craft production by the early 17th century.[10] Jesuit fathers also instituted weaving workshops called *obrajes* (S.) throughout South America to produce utilitarian articles such as cotton sail cloth and plain woolen yardage, as well as ecclesiastical garments and textiles for the Spanish nobility. These *obrajes* represent the first attempt by the Europeans to utilize the weaving skills that the indigenous people had already mastered, blending them with Old World manufacturing approaches and design ideas.

It is probable that traditional pattern manuals were brought from Europe, providing models for decoration on furniture and architecture, as well as for costume.[11] Many Colonial tapestries displayed heraldic shields, referring ornamentally to Europe's royal history. The Hapsburg, or double-headed, eagle (Plate 8, bottom) spread throughout Central and South America. The fleur-de-lis and flowered vases alluded to the Bourbon era.[12] Similar designs are evident in some early Lake Titicaca region Aymará textiles.

The Spanish also introduced new materials and methods: linen, silk, metallic yarns and, most important, sheep's wool. The European-style treadle loom made it possible to weave common cloth in a more rapid and mechanized manner (Illus. 4). This type of loom is still used all over Bolivia to make the coarse woolen fabric known as *bayeta* (S.), which is tailored into everyday garments.

Among the earliest documented Bolivian weavings are the so-called "Jesuit strip *ponchos*," woven on treadle

Illus. 4: A Potolan man weaving *bayeta* cloth on a Spanish-style treadle loom.

Illus. 5: Detail of an early "Jesuit strip *poncho*."

looms in such *obrajes* (Illus. 5). A single long strip of weaving was cut into sections of equal length, and stitched together side by side to form the completed garment. A separately woven fringe was then added on all four edges as a decorative border.[13]

It is possible that Spanish taste and design were also a factor in the evolution of the elegant *altiplano poncho* sometimes referred to as *balandrán* (S. for "cassock"). The special prerogative of Indian village priests and dignitaries, such garments were made to cover the entire body and legs. Their exceptionally large size emphasized broad plain-weave stripes in a tastefully orchestrated range of subdued colors, combined with narrow bands of complementary-warp patterning (Plate 9, top). The Colonial élite, however, preferred unpatterned *ponchos* and large scarves of rare vicuña as an indication of their status.

It is interesting to note that Spanish colonialism widely affected textile production throughout the New World, modifying the already existing styles of Central America, Mexico and the American Southwest. The influence of European design elements on both the Mexican Saltillo-style *sarape* (S., "blanket/cape") of the era from ca. 1725 to 1850 and later Navajo blankets, paralleled the Hispanic effects on certain textile patterns and costume fashions in Peru and Bolivia during the same period.

Historical Changes in Costume

The degree of Hispanicization of Indian dress styles depended greatly on both social position and the amount of contact with Colonial settlers in the developing cities. Local Indian headmen (*curacas,* Q./S.) were appointed to administer labor and agricultural policies, and were allowed to adopt certain elements of European dress. During the late 16th century, laws were passed prohibiting the use of the royal Inca-type garments or headdresses. Eventually, styles typical of the Spanish commoner were imposed on all Indian males.

Nevertheless, Indians of lesser rank continued to utilize some native dress, at the same time adopting tight knee-length trousers (*pantalones,* S.) like those worn by Spanish soldiers and short jackets (*chaquetas,* S.) of a kind popular at the Spanish court.[14] Such garments can still be seen in many Bolivian Aymará communities. In the Department of Potosí, three-cornered hats of Napoleonic origin were copied, while near Sucre the Tarabucan Indians have devised a decorated, molded leather version of the Conquistadores' armored helmet (Illus. 6). Ordinary *ponchos* of moderate size and simple design became the most characteristic feature of the highland men's costume, and continue to be seen throughout Bolivia and Peru.

Other units of male costume retained from pre-Conquest times are the small pouch (*chuspa,* Q.) used for carrying *coca* (Q./S.) leaves (chewed as a stimulant) and the pointed knit cap with earflaps (*chullo,* Q.), donned even under modern brimmed hats.

Among the women of Bolivia, differences in costume reflect the isolation of many rural communities from urban influences. In the highlands, although they have tended to cling more tenaciously to older traditions, by

Illus. 6: Two Tarabucan men and a woman display European-influenced headgear.

now they have also mixed many classic pre-Columbian prototypes with some aspects of Spanish dress.

The emergence of a new ethnic group, the *mestizos* (S.), those of mixed Indian and Spanish blood, also affected costume developments. The *mestizos'* aspiration for greater social mobility and economic freedom has prompted them to model their clothes, religion and attitudes on those of the Europeans. These people, who have moved closer to the cities and who wear contemporary clothing, are more colloquially called *cholos/cholas* (S.). The women are easily recognizable by their full-pleated skirt (*pollera,* S.), machine-made fringed shawl (*rebozo,* S.) and ubiquitous "bowler" hats.[15]

THE RELIGIOUS BACKGROUND

Religious practice during the Colonial era retained much of the magical and animistic basis of earlier popular beliefs. Worship of mountains, springs and other natural phenomena could not be fully eradicated even after the collapse of the Inca dynasty. Thus, many pre-Columbian religious forms were absorbed into local Church observances;[16] a syncretic kind of Christianity developed, with an identification between God and Inti (the Sun), or between the Virgin Mary and the fertility goddess Pacha Mama (Mother Earth).[17] It was only by the mid-17th century that native notions of divinity, such as Inti or the creator-god Viracocha, had been repressed sufficiently for Catholicism to be embraced by the Indians.

At the present time, Aymarás still maintain that supernatural beings exist everywhere.[18] Similarly, various classes of spirits populate the universe of the Quechuas. A composite of indigenous beliefs is overlaid by reluctantly adopted Christian tenets. Yet these are all integrated into social and economic relationships, as well as into daily and festive rituals, thus forming the Indians' world view. Alongside magical curing activities, supernatural beings and *huacas* (S.; earth shrines inhabited by spirits) are linked to their "most practical . . . objectives."[19]

There is little documentation either for the transformation of Quechua mythology from Inca through Colonial times,[20] or for a body of formal myths among the Aymarás. Most of the folktales that are recounted deal with animals or the origins of forms and elements in nature. Perhaps we can relate such stories to motifs in the weavings, but the connections are at times remote.

CONTEMPORARY WEAVING TRADITIONS; DESIGN MOTIFS AND THEIR MEANINGS

The first aspects of these beautiful weavings that attract our attention are their imaginative graphic patterns—birds, llamas, mice, geometric stylizations and stripes, etc. An attempt to determine their sense poses the questions of how they relate to the daily lives and religious beliefs of the people who made them, what they symbolize, and whether they signify gods and spirits, herbal and medical lore, peoples' dreams, visions of priests and sorcerers, or ancient myths. How did it occur to the weavers to combine all these elements so freely and inventively?

When the Indians are questioned about the actual interpretation of the designs, the response is often vague. Some say that the patterns were learned from childhood, and represent their village's customary style; others remark that the forms and methods were merely perpetuated by rote, and that their background has been lost or forgotten.

All over the world, we observe the continual transitions and reinterpretations that symbols undergo throughout time. A true symbol encompasses many paradoxically opposite elements, and must be viewed on both collective and individual levels to be fully comprehended. A symbol's complete meaning may never be discovered, but its explanation depends on the attitudes of those who both use and contemplate it. When symbols evolve into signs, they tend to designate more familiar, material qualities or more concrete things. Repeated use can also cause symbols to degenerate into signs, and empty structures may be all that survives of older and deeper meanings. Even traditional myths and folktales may be at variance with the actual vernacular use of symbols and signs.[21]

One theory regarding the combination of geometric and anthropomorphic patterns seen on early matrimonial garments (Plate 12, bottom) is that they may represent a pictorial code alluding to events such as marriages between families from different villages.[22] Yet it seems obvious that much of what we find on the textiles today *is* more sign than symbol, a diminished echo of what once had more profound significance. In recent decades Indian weavers have continued to observe their rural surroundings, while wryly incorporating evidence of their encounter with the modern urban world, picturing trucks, trains, helicopters, airplanes and guitars (Plate 19, top; Plate 30, top).

Note on Dating. It is not easy to establish a clear chronology of development for Bolivia's weaving traditions. The oldest textiles illustrated here date back at least a hundred years (Plate 7, bottom; Plate 9, top; Plate 10, top; Plates 11-14), but previously unexplored areas are now yielding even earlier heirlooms. Heavy daily wear in extreme weather conditions, separation from original owners or makers, and inadequate records of provenances in local or foreign museums, are among the obstacles to adequate ascription of the textiles to specific periods.

WEAVING: TRAINING, MATERIALS, METHODS

Training

Despite the weavers' passing attention to contemporary life and its conveniences, weaving itself maintains the ancient traditions of South America, just as the life around the weaving is a continuation of that honored past. The production of articles for family use is still a priority. Bolivians have not oriented themselves toward the weaving of textiles for commercial purposes. All of the family members participate in the weaving process. Young children are allowed to tend the herds of llamas and sheep; at an early age many boys and girls learn to spin on toy spindles.[23] Men as well as women ply the wool, and both sexes are involved with the dyeing. Women, however, do most of the finer handloom weaving, while men operate the upright treadle looms for the *bayeta* yardage and sometimes also knit the woolen caps (*chullos*).

Before adolescence girls learn to weave from their mothers. The looms are placed outside in the sun, as it would be impossible to see clearly in the smoke-filled, windowless interiors of the crude dwellings. The weaving activity is alternated with the countless other duties of home or farm. The most favorable time of year for textile making is the winter, between the end of harvest and the start of the next planting season (from June or July to October, in the Southern Hemisphere). A

Illus. 7: A mother and daughter from Charasani demonstrate the weaving of a *lliclla.*

daughter observes carefully, learning to set up a warp and to produce her own weaving attempts, using her mother's finished product as a model (Illus. 7).

While there is no evidence that the mature weavers prepare preliminary patterns for entire pieces, they do memorize a variety of local motifs, styles and preferred colors, and are completely familiar with the technical manipulations possible on their looms. All this they convey to the beginner. In the Potolo Region, however, small, rough "practice samplers" (called *sakas*, Q.) are created to teach the methods for forming the specific animal, bird or abstract designs that are associated with that vicinity (Figs. 19–23).

A great deal of design improvisation takes place right on the loom, within the limits of traditional methods. A weaver never produces two identical pieces. Throughout her life, a woman is motivated to continue creative innovations in her textiles. As she makes a store of special pieces for her dowry, her weaving skill may aid in attracting a husband, as it did in Inca times. Her normal role as wife and mother is complemented by the special task of weaving. Later in life, she gains increasing respect for her more attractively designed pieces, which are reserved for annual festival use and are hidden away in trunks during the rest of the year. In some areas, women are buried in their finest costume as a symbol of their dignity and achievement.

Fibers

In contemporary highland weaving, the most common fibers used are alpaca and llama hair, and sheep's wool. (Technically speaking, only sheep have "wool," but the hair of the cameloids is also frequently referred to as wool.) Alpacas and llamas can only survive at high altitudes. Since a family's wealth and well-being often depend on its herds, a symbiotic relationship exists between the animals and the people in their remote dwelling places. This is illustrated poignantly in the words of a Quechua shepherd's song to his flock:

> Because you eat, we eat,
> Because you drink, we drink,
> Because you are, we are.[24]

Alpaca fiber is favored for its silky, long hairs; when spun and woven, it produces an appealing sheen. It is often used in its natural shades as the weft, in combination with a strong wool warp; but it, too, may serve as the warp. Llama fiber is heavier and more oily, and is generally employed for knitting or for such articles as rope, slings and the large sacks called *costales* (S.) used for transporting fertilizer, grain and produce. It comes in the same natural colors as alpaca (see Illus. 8). Vicuña, an extremely soft cameloid fiber, was highly prized in the Andes. Once used exclusively by the Inca emperor, it was later an insignia for Spanish superiority. This fragile animal was hunted to near extinction in Colonial times. It is now a protected species.

Sheep's wool is currently more available than any other raw material. When well spun, it is difficult to distinguish from alpaca, and can be dyed any color. Ironically, the cost of bulk alpaca in local markets is prohibitive for

Illus. 8: A llama caravan in Potolo carrying *costales* full of grain.

Indian weavers, as it is an important export item. Now synthetics such as orlon, rayon and acrylic machine-spun yarns are appearing in the cities, and are at times substituted for the natural fibers. Although cotton was the earliest native fiber to be used in South American weavings, it does not satisfy the highlanders' needs for warmth and strength, and is rarely used alone. It is sometimes found in combination with wool, to vary the texture and pattern possibilities in certain articles (Plates 25 and 28; Fig. 25).

Spinning

One of the most notable features of Bolivian textiles is the dexterity and fineness with which the yarn has been spun. From pre-Columbian times this has been accomplished by means of the simplest of implements, the drop spindle, composed of a single stick and a balancing whorl at the bottom (Illus. 9). Preparation of the fibers for spinning includes the removal of foreign material and washing. In some parts of Bolivia, use is made of a carder called the *karkinchu* (Q.), made from a teasel plant.[25] Three stages can be outlined in the production of the finished yarn. Wisps of the fiber are selected from a ball of crude wool or hair, and are fed onto a light spindle (the *puchka;* Q. and A.) as it is turned and dropped simultaneously. This initial step creates a single strand. Secondly, the yarn is plied with two strands twisted together on a slightly larger spindle called a *k'anti* (Q.). Finally, a third spin causes the yarn to twist back on itself tightly. This "overspinning" is responsible for the extremely thin threads, durability and smooth appearance of Bolivian textiles.

Occasionally, a refined spinning technique is used to create a herringbone effect in the fabrics. The strands of yarn are spun and plied in alternating directions. The more common thread is Z-spun (clockwise, to the right) and S-plied (counterclockwise, to the left). Conversely, the S-spun thread (counterclockwise), called *lloq'e,* or "left" in Quechua, is Z-plied (clockwise). This *lloq'e* is thought to possess magical properties, and is used as an amulet to repel evil.[26] One Aymará practice for expelling spirits that have entered the body is the performance of the *cekarpayaña* (literally, "left-handify"). It involves the ritual of backward spinning, a reversal of the normal activity.[27] The pairing of S and Z-plied warp threads not only keeps the fabric from curling, but is also believed to reiterate the balance of forces in nature.[28]

Dyes and Dyeing

Traditional methods of creating colors from animal, vegetable and mineral substances date back to ancient times (ca. 3000–2500 B.C.). In many early examples, the three primary colors—red, yellow and blue—were also admixed, yielding a gamut of subtle tertiary shades. Some of these tints were produced with materials that continued to be used until the early 20th century in Bolivia. Red was created with cochineal (made from certain dried insects) or from a plant related to madder (*Relbunium*); blues were made from indigo, and yellow from a great variety of sources.[29] The proper understanding of the whole process of dyeing—from knowledge of plant cycles and habitats, to geography, dye-bath timing and temperature, fiber variations and mordants—became a true art and science in the Andes.[30] From the evidence in the Quechua language of a complex terminology for all aspects of dyeing,[31] it must have been an esteemed activity in itself.

The use of natural dyes seems to have reached its peak

Illus. 9: A Charasani woman using the traditional drop spindle.

by about 1825, and was continued skillfully for approximately another hundred years. Some dye shades no doubt had arrived earlier, with the Spanish. The *altiplano* provided shrubs and lichens, including a species of cactus called *airampu* (*Opuntia soehrensii*), whose seeds produce lovely tints from pink to red. One shade of yellow, *yareta,* was made from an *altiplano* grass (a low-growing rosette plant) that still grows in Pacajes Province and is burned as fuel. Another yellow was made from *misikú* and *molle* (Q.) (*Schinus molle*). Yellowish browns, based on lichens, have been identified as *uraq-awa,* or "bark of the earth," and *q'alaq'awa* (Q.), or "rock leather," but their present use has not been verified. Some shades of violet are still obtained from the *capina,* a purple-skinned potato (*Solanum tuberosum*).[32] Among the Aymarás, potatoes and textiles may even share the same name, such as the *patikal'a* (A.), a varicolored tuber whose name also signifies a multihued fabric.[33] The lush vegetation in mountain valleys yielded many kinds of plants, such as platanillo leaves (*Indigo suffruticosa*) for blues and elderberry (*Sambucus nigra*) for purples.

The dyes are made fast with several possible mordants. Alum (from aluminum sulfate found in rocks) is the one most frequently used. Also employed are lime and lemon juices, *chicha* (fermented corn beer) and urine. The yarn may be dyed before or after spinning. Placed in a clay or iron pot, it is boiled from several hours to a day, depending on the dye and the desired color saturation. Chemical aniline dyes, called *brillantes* (S.) by the Indians, were first imported into Bolivia by way of Peru late in the 19th century. They became popular because of their bright colors and the obvious time and labor-saving factors. They can be seen for sale in powdered form in virtually every village marketplace, and have almost completely replaced the natural substances.

Few weavers now recall more than one or two natural color sources or dye methods. The ones most commonly mentioned are *nogal,* the bark, roots or leaves of the walnut tree (*Juglans neotropica*), for golds and browns; and household soot (*carbón*) for blacks and browns.

A resist dye technique internationally known as *ikat* (*watado* in Quechua)[34] is sometimes used to decorate textiles in several regions. The village of Ulla Ulla, outside of Charasani, seems to specialize in warp-*ikat* patterning (Plate 2). The villages of Calcha and Caiza in the Department of Potosí also produce *ponchos* with this form of design (Plates 21, top, and 22, top). Occasionally *alforjas* (saddlebags, S.) with *ikat* patterning are found, such as the one appearing in Fig. 12.

We may regret the inevitable demise of knowledge about the organic dyes and the old techniques. Nevertheless, the contemporary weavers continue to bring originality and skill to their adaptation of new materials.

Looms

As with all other elements of Andean weaving, the structural design of looms has been quite consistent since pre-Columbian times. They are built simply, with readily available rustic materials that are often passed down by a mother to her daughter along with her weaving style. In the absence of a precise Quechua word for loom, the

Illus. 10: A Potolan woman weaving a *poncho* on a staked horizontal loom.

Weaving Techniques

Before weaving can begin, the warp, or lengthwise yarn, must be arranged in a specific way. A continuous length of yarn is wound in a figure-eight pattern over the parallel poles at each end of the loom. During this time-consuming process, yarns of different colors are selected (where the patterned areas will eventually form) and a careful thread count is made to insure uniformity. The sections of pattern warps are rearranged, depending on the specific weave structure chosen, before the shed rod and string heddles are inserted.[36]

The uncut warp loops at the ends of the loom and the removable string heddles make it possible to create a fabric with four selvedges. To do this, a kind of "back-weaving"[37] is employed. Working from both the top and the bottom of the loom alternately toward the middle, the weaver is finally unable to continue the design in the patterned areas, so the "backweaving" emerges as an irregular stippled or checked section, which may be called the "termination" (Fig. 1). This area can be observed in all Bolivian textiles, usually two to four inches from one end of the cloth.

Bolivian weavings are warp-faced and are noted for their complex warp patterning. After the loom has been properly warped, the weaver uses her fingers or a sharpened llama-bone implement, a *wichuña* (Q. and A.), to pick up the warp yarns of the desired colors for the design. Pattern bands of this type are called *pallay* (Q.), or "pick-up." As each row of weft yarn passes through the warps, the weaver is careful to vigorously "beat" it down into position, using a special wooden sword or llama-bone pick. The firm beating, combined with the fineness of the preliminary spinning, is largely responsible for the tightness and density of these textiles. In many of them, warp counts of well over 100 to the inch, and wefts numbering 20 to 50 per inch, surpass the finest European woolen textiles or Persian *kilims*. It may take a weaver more than six months of painstaking, intermittent work to complete a full piece.

The diversity of weave structures and techniques that have been developed in highland Bolivia is remarkable. Each locality seems to have its own preferences for certain constructions and for particular designs. The majority of the textiles are double-faced and reversible, with the same designs appearing in opposite (positive/negative and negative/positive) color combinations on each side. It is possible to point out several general structures that are used to decorate the plain-weave foundation that is common to all regions:

SUPPLEMENTARY-WARP PATTERNING can be found in the Department of La Paz, around Amarete, Ayata and Yanahuaya. Two or more colors of supplementary (additional) yarn lie between the foundation warps and are lifted to the surface to create the design. The combination of warps and "tie-down spots" causes "a mixture of longer floats on the 'wrong' side of the fabric,"[38] and so the design is not identical in appearance on both sides.

Occasionally, SUPPLEMENTARY-WEFT PATTERNING is seen in narrow hatbands, belts or *chuspas* (Plate 20, top). Areas of warp-faced plain weave form the background, overlaid by the patterning of supplementary weft "floats" in different colors.

contrivance is sometimes referred to as *ahuanakuna*, which has been translated as "warp-and-things," *ahua* (or *awa*) being the root of the verb *ahuay* (to weave), as well as the term for warp.[35] The most common loom apparatus for the weaving of patterned garments is the horizontal type, with two parallel posts staked into the ground at four corners, and two ropes to adjust the tension (Illus. 7 and 10). A variant of this type is the semi-upright or lashed-beam loom, which is propped obliquely against a wall. The width of these looms is quite small, averaging 18 to 24 inches. Thus, *llicllas* and *ponchos* are always woven in two matching oblong halves, and are then sewn together with any one of a number of ornamental stitches. The seam is called the *costura* (S.).

Back-strap looms are used primarily to make smaller cloths, headbands and belts. The weaver supplies the tension necessary to stretch the warp threads by fastening one end of the loom to a tree or post, and the other around her waist. Thus, she can slacken or tighten the tension by leaning forward or backward. In certain areas, several kinds of vertical-frame looms and plaiting frames are used to make saddle blankets, hammocks and tapestry-woven bedspreads. In most of these instances, the entire loom, or at least the warp assembly, is collapsible so that it may be rolled up and brought in out of the rain, or its position shifted to accommodate the weaver's schedule. The treadle loom, introduced by the Spanish, is the only nonindigenous device used in Bolivian textile production.

Illus. 11: Kaalaya, Charasani Valley: a typical Andean village at approximately 12,000 feet above sea level.

Many regions include the technique of DOUBLE CLOTH in their weaving repertoire, and it is commonly seen in textiles from the Charasani Valley and the Bolívar Region. This type has been described as "warp-faced 'one-weft' double cloth, with the hidden weft" used to weave "first the upper layer, then the lower one, forming a flattened tube." The interchange of warps between the faces makes the color pattern different on each side.[39]

One of the most frequent weave structures seen in Bolivia is the COMPLEMENTARY-WARP WEAVE, also called "opposites patterning."[40] Numerous variations exist within this construction, "depending on the length of the floats, their alignment, the order in which the elements of each color are placed on the loom, and the manner in which the interchange of faces is accomplished."[41]

Whichever combination of techniques is chosen for a *poncho, lliclla* or *chuspa,* the Bolivian weaver takes great pride in the detailing and embellishment of the completed fabric. Many weavings are finished with a handwoven tubular edging called a *ribete* (S.) that may also prevent the edges from fraying, though it primarily strengthens and highlights them. Many different patterns have been devised, including diagonal stripes, checks, meanders and the so-called *ojo de gato* (S., "cat's eye") with its minuscule concentric diamond shapes (Plate 10, bottom). "The warp for this edging is set up with one end attached to a stake in the ground and the other end held in the weaver's hand." The weft is on a needle, and is "sewn through the edge of the *poncho* or *lliclla* as part of the weaving process."[42] Instead of a *ribete,* many *ponchos* have a separately woven band of fringe (*fleco,* S.) sewn around their edges. Small *coca* pouches and shoulder bags often receive the most attention, being decorated with ebullient combinations of *ribetes,* tassels, pompoms, beaded scallops, dangling silver coins and finely braided straps (Plates 4, top, 6, top, and 15).

It seems almost ironic that textiles made with such elaborate weaving processes and loving attention to embellishment are destined for simple utilitarian purposes – daily wear in the countryside or the wrapping of food bundles or babies! Only the more decorative festival pieces, which are conserved for special occasions and are worn for more deliberate purposes of display, fully reveal the artistry and the amount of work involved in this exceptional weaving.

REGIONAL WEAVING CENTERS AND DIFFERENCES IN COSTUME

Department of La Paz: Charasani Valley

Bolivia is a land of extreme contrasts in climate and topography. There are vast areas of mountains and plateaux, interspersed with high valleys and gorges, and still other areas of lush tropical lowlands. Amidst the remote Andes northeast of Lake Titicaca lies the area of the Charasani Valley (Illus. 11). Ancient burial sites have given proof of man's existence there for over a thousand years.[43] Its inhabitants exemplify certain persistent traditions of Andean social organization and religion.

Even before the spread of the Inca empire, this region was renowned as the home of the Callawayas (or Qolla-huayas), a "special cultural subgroup of the Aymará nation,"[44] famed as diviners and herbal healers. The name Callawaya is derived from the Aymará terms *q'olla*, meaning "medicine," and *wayu*, or "bag"; thus: "he who carries a medicine bag."[45] This is a reference to the *alforjas* (saddlebags) still used to carry the special paraphernalia of the healers.[46] It is believed that these Indians were brought to Cuzco, Peru, to serve the royal Incas as court physicians, and that they learned the Quechua language at that time. They perfected many medical skills, including brain surgery and the use of simple forms of penicillin, Terramycin and quinine,[47] long before European medicine arrived with the Spanish. Their expertise with herbal remedies, charms, sooth-saying and esoteric rituals is still acknowledged through-out the Andes and South America.

Near the town of Charasani, dozens of small village communities known as *ayllus* are scattered across the steep slopes of the Apolobamba range. It is the Calla-wayas' physical and spiritual relationship with these mountains that forms the foundation of their society, religion and art.

The weaving, exchanging and wearing of cloth is significant in all aspects of life for these people. The ritual of first haircutting brings the young child an initial set of adult clothing.[48] Mothers instruct their daughters in weaving techniques while transmitting other traditional and ancestral lore. An accomplished weaver is a respected member of the community. At the time of marriage, the couple dresses in elaborately decorated costumes. Often a girl presents her future husband with a dowry of cloth she has woven,[49] although in some cases, her matrimonial skirt is a gift from her mother.

Cloth reflects social status and designates specific political and ritual roles; for instance, when men become village elders and leaders, or when they sponsor community festivals, they wear large, carefully wrought *ponchos*. In funeral ceremonies the dead are often wrapped in their best costumes, for it is "cold inside the earth" while the soul travels through the underground waterways toward the highlands.[50] Callawayas communicate with their dead relatives through textiles[51] by placing *coca* leaves beneath garments that once belonged to the deceased, and asking them to return. While weavings naturally fulfill functional and social needs, "on a spiritual level, clothes refer to cosmological truths through the pictographs woven into them."[52] These designs can only be understood in the light of the land and traditions that surround them.

Each community develops its own design styles within a similar overall format, as if composing woven folk songs. Charasani weavings are characterized by arrangements of extremely animated patterned bands (usually in double cloth) and plain-weave stripes of varying widths and spectrums. These colored strata correspond to the levels of land and the resources of the mountains.[53] Thus, corn and wheat grown at lower altitudes are signified by green warp threads, the median-level fields of barley and potatoes are shown by reds, and the higher grazing areas appear as maroon stripes.[54] Nevertheless, in Charasani weavings, there are few, if any, direct representations of such plants.[55]

The creative originality of these weavers is expressed by their special flair for polychrome effects. A skillful alternation of vibrantly hued stripes and figured bands typifies the attractive weavings of Charasani (Plates 1–6).

That the weavers' inspiration is also drawn from a close and appreciative observation of their environment is evident from the patterned bands (*pallay*, Q.), which are woven with a spirited array of graphic motifs—represen-tational, emblematic and abstract. Unlikely juxtaposi-tions of horses, dogs, cows, birds, chickens, mice and fish appear alongside vivacious human figures, dancing or holding garlands, as they might be seen at festivals or marriages. Stylized diamonds symbolizing the sun, *inti* (Plate 28; Fig. 1), are frequently inserted among the lozenges, chevrons, flowers and zoomorphic forms. For the people of the Charasani Valley, the mountain and all its denizens are sacred. Condors symbolize earth shrines; their natural posture, with wings lifted and spread apart, resembles the shape of a mountain and its three signi-ficant levels, from the summit down to the fields near the river (denoting the heavens, this world and the nether world). On fabrics, the condor may also serve as a metaphor of the Andeans, who, like the bird hatched in its lofty nest, are born on and return to the mountain.[56]

Several angular and curved or "hooked" variations of the scroll motif (*wajrapallay*, Q.) are said to depict the snail or cornucopia (Plate 2). These repeated, or mirror-image, triangular and "hooked-finial" designs appear on the garments of ordinary people, but are also intimately associated with the costume of the Callawaya. The term *wajra* contains two levels of meaning: on the material plane it encourages prosperity and joy, while in the spiritual realm it connotes supernatural powers.[57] The *poncho* in Plate 5, the *capacho* (S., man's shoulder bag) in Plate 4, bottom, and one *chuspa* in Plate 6 all bear such designs, which may signify the wearer's mastery of magical, divinatory or curing methods and knowledge. One motif, formed by two or three concentric lozenges edged with striations, is said to refer to the "eyes of one who knows how to see"—that is, the Callawaya himself.[58] A greater number of pattern bands (eight to 12 per piece), containing a lively diversity of graphics, is the mark of a superior weaving.

In the villages of this area, the more extensively decorated *ponchos* (Plate 5) are greatly valued and infrequently woven. More typically, women make *llicllas* for their own daily or festival wear, or simple striped and less colorful plain-weave *ponchos* for mundane use by the men. The elementary shapes and uncut, untailored aspects of Bolivian weavings provide flexibility of movement for the wearers, and give them free rein to

Illus. 12: A Charasani family wearing *poncho, lliclla, wincha, chullo* and regional hats.

Illus. 13: Three women at a festival in Charasani, wearing fine *llicllas.*

further adorn themselves with such accessories as hand-woven sashes and pouches, silver ornaments, flowers, hats, encircled with rickrack, and beaded headbands (Illus. 12 and 13).

This headband (*wincha*) is used only in the Charasani area, and is exclusively the province of women (Plates 3, top, and 4, top). During the ritual of first haircutting, the girl's head is wrapped with *winchas* belonging to her grandmothers. The depictions of flora and fauna are a "representational magic which provides the wearer with fertility." The headband itself signifies the lineage and power of females in the family.[59]

Department of La Paz: Lake Titicaca Region and the Altiplano — Pacajes and Copacabana

The terrain of northwestern Bolivia is primarily high tableland (13,000 ft.) known as the *altiplano*. It is an extensive but inhospitable territory of approximately 38,000 square miles, with little rain, few trees and an immense solitude.[60] Yet for centuries it has been Bolivia's largest population center, first called Collasuyu by the Incas, then named Collao by the Spaniards.

Bolivia's northern border with Peru bisects Lake Titicaca, the world's highest navigable lake at 12,500 feet. Ancient cosmological myths refer to the lake as the birthplace of the sun, where the sun god created the early races of men, including the Inca dynasty itself.[61] The ruins of the monolithic stone temples of Tiahuanaco, located near the former shores of the lake, attest to its religious importance.

Although no very large cities have evolved around the lake, there are many villages where antique textiles were made. Since it is difficult to assign an exact provenance to such heirloom weavings, the term "Lake Region textile" has been used to describe the products of this area. They may be characterized by broad solid fields of black, brown or gray plain weave, with very thin pattern bands featuring tiny geometric designs (Plate 7, bottom).

Even before Bolivia gained its independence in 1825, the Lake Region produced textiles of exquisite fineness. They were made by Aymará groups in and around Puno and Juli (now in Peru), as well as in other villages on the Bolivian side of Lake Titicaca as far south as Oruro. The exceptionally "tight" weaving, and the range of subtly muted and clear vegetal-dyed hues in these textiles, are a triumph of artistic expression.

Within the Department of La Paz lies the Province of Pacajes, near the border between Peru and Chile. This area was an important one prior to Inca times, and Francisco Pizarro appointed himself to its leadership when he and his troops arrived in Bolivia around 1540.[62] The elevated, dry plains are well suited to the grazing of cameloids. The Aymará Indians of the region became noted for their masterly spinning and weaving of naturally dyed alpaca fibers, although current production does not rival the beauty and fineness of the earlier work.

The village chieftains (hilacatas) wore a costume that included a small ponchito and a large poncho called a challapata, usually folded and fastened over the shoulder. These noble garments have zones of finely spun black alpaca, alternated with soft natural dye colors such as rose, ultramarine and burgundy. They show very little patterning, although they make frequent use of S and Z-plied threads near the borders of each side. In contrast to the simplicity of these larger pieces, Pacajes belts display a profusion of inventively manipulated geometric, anthropomorphic and zoomorphic forms (Plate 8, top).

The women's garments included the lustrous, dark alpaca skirt (urku, A.) and the lliclla, made in wide sections of brown or black, with narrow bands of paler tones. The more boisterous colors of the broad belt imparted vitality to an otherwise somber costume.

Along the eastern shore of Lake Titicaca, the town of Copacabana has been an important pilgrimage center to Catholic-converted Indians for over three hundred years. It is possible that ponchos such as the one in Plate 8, bottom, were made in this area. Its designs are eclectic, and include many typical Aymará devices, though magnified in scale. Also notable is the bold use of red and green on a natural tan field.

Department of Potosí: Bolívar Region

Within the 13 provinces of the Department of Potosí in southern Bolivia, a wide variety of weaving styles may be distinguished. Its center, the city of Potosí, was founded in 1545, when silver deposits were discovered inside the Cerro Rico mines (13,500 feet). For two centuries it produced an unprecedented amount of wealth, and the city became the largest and most exploited in the New World. Great numbers of Indian and Negro laborers were imported to extract the precious metal. The ethnic diversity of the present population reflects that work force.

Northwest of Potosí, and spanning the southern border of the Department of Cochabamba, is the Bolívar Region. This isolated, mountainous location has been identified as the source of some of the most beautiful antique costumes in Bolivia. The Indians of this locale appear to have originally been members of the Laris group of Aymará-speakers. They observed the Aymará tradition of handing down ceremonial and matrimonial garments to their children.

Early Bolívar textiles are immediately singled out by their attractive natural tints and uncluttered compositions. Subtle but sophisticated color schemes evolved, based on the use of pink and purple vegetal dyes. The medium-size ponchos once worn by village headmen are scarce. A background of predominantly pink/magenta, or indigo plain weave, separates thin contiguous bands of double-cloth designs (Plate 13). Recurrent motifs in these stripes, which also appear in the very fine chuspas (Plate 14) and in aksus, are the lymi linku and lymi tika, stylized floral vines common to the area.

The old matrimonial costumes of Bolívar-area women are among the rarest and most beautiful in all of the Andes. Families who have inherited the few that do exist, now rent the attire to young couples for their weddings, so that they may still observe the old dress traditions. The large cape-like aksus in Plate 10, top, and Plate 11 are stunning examples of visual and technical refinement. The spectrum of hues is subdued, ranging from speckled browns and pinks to violets, with highlights of blue and gold. The horizontal colored stripes of plain weave are alternated with thin auxiliary bands of geometric or figurative designs, executed in various complementary-warp or double-cloth techniques (Plate 12, bottom). Companion belts (Plate 12, top) and llicllas echo similar designs and tonalities.

Though located in remote areas, these Aymará Indians appear to have been greatly influenced by contact with neighboring Quechua tribes. Early in the 20th century, perhaps owing to local economic and political factors, the prevailing language shifted from Aymará to Quechua. With this change came a complete alteration of weaving designs, techniques and materials. Knowledge of natural dyeing was supplanted by use of synthetic colors; even the combinations chosen differed greatly from the earlier preferences. Most typical now are groupings of purple, maroon, orange and green. All of these may appear together as well, set beside wider zones of intense clear red or black. This palette may seem strident, but the combinations are novel and bold.

Ceremonial ponchos and aksus ceased to be made, and a new style of decoration evolved on the lliclla (Plate 16 and Fig. 10). The designs created in broad panels of warp-faced doubled cloth were referred to as kurti (Q.), and seem to represent a transitional period dating at least to the 1940s.[63] Attractive wide belts (Plate 17) also display this later phase of Bolívar design, characterized by vigorous representations of paired condors with flaring wings, S-shaped "snakes," sun symbols and small chevrons, flowers or spirals. As omens often govern the Indians' behavior and activities, the frequent appearance of condors bears out a belief that "to see a condor while planting means good fortune."[64] Similarly patterned textiles are also associated with the vicinity of Challa, in southwest Cochabamba, perhaps by way of commercial links with Bolívar.

Department of Potosí: Macha and Pocoata

In northern Potosí several different weaving styles have developed in close proximity to each other. Within the Province of Chayanta, roads are often impassable in the rainy season, and isolated hamlets have retained their distinctive characteristics. Textiles from the town of Macha are always geometrically oriented. Its most ornate garment is the woman's lliclla (Plates 18 and 19, bottom), in which rows of stripes contain chevrons and/or diamonds full of tiny octagonal or circular shapes that produce a flickering mosaic effect. The background colors, with a few exceptions, are somber tones, with minimal highlights of red, yellow, orange and lavender. The men's costume is Spanish-influenced, featuring knee pants, a vest and a jacket of homespun cloth, adorned with sash (Plate 20, top) and chuspa.

The village of Pocoata produces weavings generally identified by the use of a complementary-warp technique sometimes called "pebble weave." The designs may be either geometric (Plate 20, bottom) or figurative (Plate 19, top; Fig. 11). Animals such as birds, rodents and cows are depicted enclosed in sections of the patterned bands. *Llicllas* and *aksus*, as well as belts and bags, are the weavings on which this decoration occurs (Plates 30 and 32, bottom).

Department of Potosí: Calcha and Caiza

South of the city of Potosí, another area creates weavings that are visually dazzling and of excellent technical quality. Villages such as Calcha, Vitichi and Yawisla are noted for garments of very finely spun wool. The women from these communities wear a black dress (*almilla*, S.), relieved by lavish embroidery on the billowing sleeves. Their black *aksus* are bordered with narrow bands of busy, compact geometric designs, which lend them an electrical tension. A long, thin belt is wrapped around the waist.

The Calcha man's costume is dominated by his striking *poncho*, made in several styles. The *pante poncho* is named after its prevalent burgundy background color; it is articulated with delicate, slim strips of geometrics in complementary warp, as well as with thin areas of *ikat*. A black *poncho* with a few dark red bands is known as the *luto* (S.), referring to the practice of wearing dark clothes when mourning.[65] The gay, multicolored *ponchos* with stripes of even width have been termed *banderas* or *bolivianos*, perhaps for their resemblance to the segmentations of a flag (Plate 21). The hues range from muted combinations to the more prismatic "rainbows." All of these types of *ponchos* are typically decorated near their borders with areas of warp-*ikat* patterning, a technique especially characteristic of the Calcha area (Plate 21, top). These evenly measured banded patterns may appear somewhat static when the textiles are displayed flat, but Calcha men often wear their *ponchos* folded or draped casually over the shoulders, allowing the cloth to flow gracefully with the contours of the body in motion.

The nearby village of Caiza is also known for the production of *ikat*-decorated *ponchos* (Plate 22, top). These *ponchos* differ in size and scale from those made in Calcha. Other kinds of Caiza weavings are *llicllas* and *ponchos*, made in stripes of plain weave interspersed with complementary-warp geometric designs.

Department of Potosí: Potolo Region

Elsewhere in the Department of Potosí, and crossing into Chuquisaca, the inhabitants have developed a more freely imaginative and pictorial approach to textile decoration. It contrasts to the rather formal, abstracting and symmetrical styles of other areas in this district. The Potolo Region extends over many barren miles, its rolling countryside sparse in vegetation. Many primitive family compounds (*estancias*, S.), comprising adobe huts and rock-enclosed corrals, are the only human incursions onto this remote landscape (Illus. 14).

Potolo weavings are conceived in a truly pictorial

Illus. 14: Small family ranches scattered over the barren landscape of the Potolo Region.

fashion. Adjustments are made in the placement of the figures within patterned zones to reveal their forms while the garment is being worn. There is an infinite variety of individual design solutions and combinations within a similar compositional structure.

The *aksu* is woven in two separate pieces, which are joined together by discreet stitching. The top section is then either pinned over the shoulders or rolled under a belt, and is usually only partially decorated (Fig. 18). The lower half is fully decorated, and often suggests the narrative aspects of an illustration. The customary format displays three bands of designs. The top and bottom registers are parallel, and repeat a nearly identical sequence of figures; while the wider central panel frames another parade of animals, usually distributed more loosely, or placed askew. Within this basic format, each Potolo *aksu* displays the weaver's unique ingenuity and creativity.

Offsetting the complexity of designs in Potolan weavings, the choice of colors is restrained. Black or brown serves as the recessive background in *ponchos*, *aksus* and *llicllas* (Illus. 15). The patterned areas are woven in shades of red and maroon (and now, bright pinks), occasionally punctuated by blue or green.

The man's main festival garment is the handsome *capote poncho*. Its broad patterned bands offer the weaver an expanded field for design improvisation. Long, non-

Illus. 15: A Potolan woman wearing a *lliclla*.

repetitive lines of animals are frequently seen in symmetrical or complementary pairs (Plate 23; Fig. 13). In addition to the *poncho* there is a special *chuspa* woven with the same colors and animal figures, decorated with long wrapped yarn streamers ending in pompoms.

The practice of burying the dead in their most treasured weavings has limited the traces of 19th-century or earlier textiles, making it equally difficult to outline a definite chronology of Potolo development. However, some general stylistic devices can be observed which may tentatively establish several historical phases. In the oldest pieces, a few approaches have been distinguished:

(1) Regular rows of the same animal (often a long-tailed rodent, the *viscacha*, Q./S.) in miniature scale are arranged to fill the entire bottom section of an *aksu*. The number of figures may range from dozens to hundreds in a single textile of this type.

(2) Another version consists of many one-of-a-kind creatures, which vary in scale and are juxtaposed irregularly in space. Inserted between these primary forms are secondary, smaller animals (diminutive birds, mice, rabbits or owls) whose directional orientation often differs from that of the larger ones.

(3) Occasionally *aksus* and *ponchos* were decorated solely with geometric patterns, their chief symbol being the diamond-shaped *inti* motif.

In all of these early weavings, the spinning is uniformly fine. The delineation of the animals is crisp and delicate, and they seem to possess a personality, or an inner life, of their own.

After about 1950, the forms in the compositions were floated more asymmetrically, though still dynamically. During the past 10 to 15 years, the younger women have not had the time to contrive the more intricate, original designs, nor have they felt "the keen competitive weaving urge of their elders."[66] While recent weavings do incorporate many features from the past, in most contemporary pieces the rows of coarser zoomorphic forms are somewhat rigidly aligned, often mimicking each other more monotonously than in older examples. Yet the repetition of a single bird may also create the effect of migratory flocks flying in formation, or the duplication of one type of beast may be interpreted as grazing herds. These are both frequent sights in the highland areas.

Undoubtedly the most enigmatic of Bolivian textiles in their iconography, Potolan weavings are recognized by their inventive, often playful, diversity of stylized animals and figures. Their impact immediately reminds the viewer of the marvelous mythical beings found on many ancient Peruvian burial cloths and regal tapestries. It is not unreasonable to suppose that as Quechua Indians were brought south into Bolivia, first by the Incas, then by the Spaniards, they recalled the mythological and traditional sources from which they continued to draw vestiges of inspiration. Yet today, when questioned about the precise significance or symbolism in their weavings, the Potolo Indians seem to be either genuinely unaware of their true meanings, or perhaps hesitant to inform anyone outside of their immediate community. The peculiar admixture of native animistic beliefs and magical practices with Christian notions of Sin, Hell and the Devil, may account for the weavers' inclination toward the bizarre and phantasmal, which is the vocabulary of Potolan design. Whatever the origins of their inspiration, it is obvious that in no other weaving area do we see such spontaneous freedom of figurative expression or such visionary qualities in pattern arrangement and motifs. Ultimately, the interpretation of these intriguing compositions and their symbology is left to the viewer's imagination.

The repertory of designs is impressive. Some garments are dominated by large, voracious bird-like creatures whose bellies contain smaller birds (Plate 24; Fig. 17). Imaginary animals that resemble humpbacked dragons with forked tongues and arrow-pronged tails (Plate 22, bottom; Figs. 16 and 24), grimacing lions and hybrid beings referred to as *diablos* (S., devils) are also prevalent. It is possible that the double pairs of wings that are seen on some bats, owls and other fearsome birds (Plate 23) are naïvely literal attempts to portray the creatures in motion. More realistic representations of bats, quizzical dogs, felines, and antlered deer (Plate 24; Fig. 17) are also found. Saluting or equestrian human figures are infrequently portrayed (Fig. 18). But it is the magical bestiary of leering devils and animated "spirit-birds" that is the trademark and delight of Potolan textiles. From this integration of fantasy and fact emerge a vernacular language and an art that are original and complex (Illus. 16 and 17).

Department of Chuquisaca: Tarabuco Region

The modern Department of Chuquisaca in south central Bolivia was established early during the Spanish Conquest. Its fertile, sheltered valley location and moderate climate made this an appealing alternative to the harsh confines of La Paz or the mountainous Potosí mining district. The city of Chuquisaca, later renamed Sucre in honor of the liberator General Antonio José de Sucre, became a center of politics, religion and the arts by the end of the seventeenth century and is still the nation's constitutional capital.

Southeast of Sucre lies the most prominent weaving area of Chuquisaca, centered around the town of Tarabuco. Here the weekly Sunday market attracts hundreds of attractive and brightly dressed Tarabucan Indians, who travel from their outlying villages and farms. The origin of this group is very obscure, though perhaps it can be traced to a culture called the Yamparas, dating back to about 1000 A.D.[67] It is equally possible that these Indians are descended from Quechua-speaking immigrants who were forcibly brought south during the Inca reign. Today they are an energetic, proud people who have developed a costume that is unusual yet clearly registers the impact of Spanish Colonial styles.

Perhaps the most noticeable item of Tarabucan apparel is a black molded-leather helmet called a *montera* (S.), which emulates the Conquistadores' steel headgear. This is worn by both men and women, often trimmed with sequins, rosettes and small tassels. The women of each village also adapted a number of European-type wide-brimmed or boat-shaped hats, used for festivals (cf. Illus. 6).

The entire Tarabucan wardrobe can be identified by its striking colors. Men wear a large *poncho*, horizontally striped in gradated shades of maroon, orange and yellow (Plate 29, bottom; Illus. 6). Women's *llicllas* and some of their skirts utilize the same radiant hues (Plates 28 and 29, top). However, during periods of mourning, Tarabucans observe the Catholic custom of *luto*, the wearing of black garments in memory of the dead.

Beneath their *ponchos*, men wear a coarse woolen shirt, which until recently was woven in a distinctive twill weave, as were some women's dresses. Their loose knee-length *pantalones* are of white *bayeta* fabric. Miniature *ponchos* called *unkus* are worn on the shoulders like a yoke, or else are cinched under a wide, studded leather "money belt," and cover the hips (cf. Illus. 3). Sandals are now fashioned out of recycled automobile tires. Although the daily garments of the Tarabucan males are mainly striped plain weaves, their festival costumes incorporate profusely patterned *unkus* such as the marvelous one seen in Plates 26 and 27.

An important and beautiful accessory is the *chuspa*, or *coca*-leaf pouch (Plate 25; Fig. 25), emblazoned with rows of profiled horses or llamas.[68] Throughout Bolivia, Indian use of *coca* (*Erythroxylon coca*) is widespread. This

Illus. 16: A Potolan weaver proudly displaying her work.

Illus. 17: A brother and sister from the Potolo Region in festival dress.

plant has been savored and honored as divine since ancient times, although under Inca domination access to it was a luxury restricted to the ruling caste.[69] *Coca* is still present at all ritual and social occasions, offered to such deities as Pacha Mama (Earth Goddess). Scattered over a cloth, it is used by diviners, as it is considered to be a "green bible with millions of pages."[70] Continuously chewed by most Indians, *coca* alleviates fatigue, suppresses the appetite, promotes physical endurance, creates a mild euphoria and makes one impervious to pain. It is chiefly men who carry the *chuspa*, with its tiny flap pockets for the lime or quinua-ash catalyst; while women tend to wrap their leaves in small square cloths called *incuna* (Q.) or *tari* (A.).[71]

Highlighting the woman's costume is the straight wrap-around skirt or *aksu* (Plates 28 and 29, top; Illus. 6 and 18). Its black plain-weave top is dramatically offset by the wide bottom section, which is profusely decorated with parades of horses embedded in bold geometric designs. The use of a white cotton warp along with the thicker colored wool results in a three-dimensional textured effect in the patterned areas. Tarabucan women usually wear a *lliclla* fastened with a silver *tupo* (Q.), as in Illus. 19, or by a safety pin. Their plaited hair is decorated with long tubular-woven, or braided and tasseled ties called *tulmas* (Q.).

CONCLUSION: BOLIVIA TODAY

The regional styles of weaving illustrated here by no means represent the totality of the Bolivian textile production. Areas such as Calamarca, Challa, Sica-Sica, Ayata (Plate 32, top) and Lleque (Figs. 28–30) have already yielded significant examples of the craft. As interest and scholarship increase, important data and previously unknown types will surely be brought to the attention of researchers and will assist in filling out the historical picture. Challenging discoveries await those who will explore the rugged landscape of a country still largely untouched by technology. Weaving of the superlative quality seen in antique pieces from the Bolívar, Lake Titicaca or Pacajes Regions has unfortunately ceased to be. Those areas that do continue weaving activity cannot remain unaffected by modernization.

As in other newly developing countries around the world, change in Bolivia is imminent and inevitable. Its indigenous Indians are faced with many cultural dilemmas and are succumbing to long-term social pressures. Since the Agrarian Reform Act of 1952, many facets of the age-old Indian way of life have been disrupted. The formation of agricultural cooperatives is drawing more and more of the rural population toward large towns and especially to the urban capital of La Paz, where they are prompted to commit themselves to trading in a money economy. Progressive commercialization of Bolivia's wealth of mineral deposits will propel the nation into the future, and will again rely heavily on Indian labor. Even the most inaccessible settlements will eventually be reached as improved roads and communications networks are constructed.

For hundreds of years, Bolivia's native population has formed part of a social order that regrettably has

Illus. 18: A Tarabucan woman wearing a fine *aksu,* a *lliclla* and a *montera* hat.

Illus. 19: An elderly woman in traditional Tarabucan dress (note *tupo* pin).

overlooked or devalued much of their cultural and artistic tradition. The younger generations of Quechuas and Aymarás will be obligated to attend schools where not only the subjects, but the Spanish language itself, will dissociate them from their parents, their communities and the influences of their ethnic heritage. As young men leave their homes, venturing into the big cities to find work, religious, esthetic and herbal-healing traditions once held sacred are no longer transmitted and are soon forgotten.

These negative factors notwithstanding, Bolivian weavers have been able to fashion incomparable textiles. Our selection and assessment of these works are offered to acquaint the reader with their history and manner of production, and to celebrate this remarkable achievement. It is possible that some encouragement to continue the tradition and maintain high levels of quality may be felt by the weavers themselves as a wider audience appreciates their work. To the authors, they have displayed their inherent talents and skills, their astute sense of color and design and their joy in creating beautiful garments with which to decorate themselves and their surroundings. Perhaps their example may provide us with new dimensions of inspiration and stimulate outlets for creative expression in our own lives.

NOTES

For full titles and other bibliographical data, see entries under authors' names in the Bibliography that follows.

1. Osborne, *South American Mythology*, p. 14.
2. Rowe, p. 11.
3. Osborne, *Indians of the Andes*, p. 10.
4. Weil, p. 79; Osborne, *Indians of the Andes*, p. 10.
5. Osborne, *South American Mythology*, p. 31.
6. *Ibid.*, p. 28.
7. Kubler, p. 363.
8. *Ibid.*; also cited by Adelson & Takami, p. 10.
9. Rigoberto Paredes, p. 22.
10. Kubler, p. 348.
11. Kelemen, discussing Guatemalan weaving in "The Weaver's High Art," p. 6, supports our own supposition about the appearance of such pattern manuals in North and South America, when he states: "Pattern books for handwork were widely distributed. Sample albums, printed as far away as Poland, found their way into the convents of the New World, often carried by newly arriving nuns and priests. Thus certain embroidery motifs favored in Latin America appear very like those in Central Europe."
12. Cavallo, p. 182.
13. Higgins & Kenny, p. 5, Plate 1, suggest that their example dates to 1760. See also Rowe, Fig. 38, for a similar textile, dated late 18th to early 19th century.
14. Olen, p. 233 (this was in the 16th century).
15. Weil, p. 85. It is believed that these "bowler" hats were first introduced in the early 20th century, when they were inadvertently shipped from England to South America, then sold to the Bolivians, becoming quite popular!
16. Mishkin, p. 462.
17. Osborne, *Indians of the Andes*, pp. 227-8.
18. Tschopik, p. 570.
19. Mishkin, p. 462.
20. Kubler, p. 406.
21. Wasserman, p. 21 (based on the thinking of Carl Jung also).
22. Tracht, Arthur, in discussion.
23. Goodell, p. 53.
24. Quoted from Cohen, television film cited.
25. Girault, p. 25; also in Meisch, p. 322.
26. Goodell, p. 53.
27. LaBarre, p. 107.
28. Cohen, television film.
29. King, Introduction.
30. Goodell, p. 54.
31. Girault, pp. 25-30; also translated in Higgins & Kenny, pp. 24-5.
32. LaBarre, p. 109; and Tracht, Arthur, field informant.
33. LaBarre, p. 107.
34. *Ikat* is the more widely used word, from the Indonesian term *mengikat*, the technique of tying off those design areas that are to remain undyed, before weaving construction. The Quechua equivalent is *watado*, from the verb *watay*, also signifying "tie" or "wrap" – but it is not in common usage, even in Bolivia. Therefore the authors have chosen to use the term that is best known to general readers.
35. Meisch, p. 325.
36. Cason & Cahlander, p. 25.
37. Meisch, p. 327; see also Cason & Cahlander, p. 158.
38. Cason & Cahlander, p. 32.
39. *Ibid.*
40. *Ibid.*, p. 33.
41. Rowe, p. 67.
42. Meisch, p. 327; see also Cason & Cahlander, pp. 125 ff., for instructions.
43. Ryden (unpaged).
44. Tschopik, p. 569.
45. LaBarre, p. 217.
46. Oblitas, p. 14.
47. *Ibid.*, p. 19.
48. Bastien, p. 103.
49. *Ibid.*, p. xvii.
50. *Ibid.*, p. 175.
51. *Ibid.*, p. 111.
52. *Ibid.*, p. 103.
53. *Ibid.*, p. 109.
54. Adelson & Takami, p. 38.
55. Girault, p. 40.
56. Bastien, p. 63.
57. Oblitas, p. 201.
58. Girault, p. 41.
59. Bastien, pp. 113-4.
60. Osborne, *Bolivia: Land Divided*, p. 8.
61. *Ibid.*, p. 9.
62. Julien, p. 12.
63. Berger, Steve, field informant.
64. Tschopik, p. 564.
65. Adelson & Takami, p. 34.
66. Yorke, Roger, personal correspondence, May 1977.
67. Rojas, Elizabeth, personal correspondence from Sucre, Bolivia, 1978.
68. It may be noted here that the typical pattern of the Tarabucan pouch, with its registers of animals seen in profile, and its composition divided down the center with a single band of contrasting or reversed colors, can also be seen in a pre-Inca prototype from Nazca, Ica, Peru, now in the collection of the Museum of the American Indian, N.Y., dated 500 A.D. (Museum #16/4816, collected by A. Hyatt Verrill). In its middle section appear similar rows of llamas, with the central band in opposite colors; its pattern attests to both the long tradition of *coca* use, and to persistent design factors.
69. Kubler, p. 394.
70. Oblitas, p. 27.
71. Tschopik, pp. 556-7.

Bibliography

Adelson, Laurie, and Takami, Bruce, *Weaving Traditions of Highland Bolivia.* Los Angeles, Craft and Folk Art Museum Catalogue, Dec. 1978.

Bastien, Joseph W., *Mountain of the Condor: Metaphor and Ritual in an Andean Ayllu.* St. Paul, West Publishing Co., 1978.

Cason, Marjorie, and Cahlander, Adele, *The Art of Bolivian Highland Weaving.* New York, Watson-Guptill, 1976.

Cavallo, Adolph S., *Tapestries of Europe and Colonial Peru in the Museum of Fine Arts, Boston.* Boston, M.F.A., 1967.

Cohen, John, *Patterns from the Past.* Television film produced for WGBH, Boston, on Q'erro Indian Life in the Peruvian Andes, for "Nova" series; broadcast on KQED, S.F., Feb. 8, 1979.

Drum, Jim, "Andean Weaving Draws on the Past," *El Palacio,* Vol. 81:4. Santa Fe, Museum of New Mexico, Winter 1975, pp. 35–45.

Emery, Irene, *The Primary Structure of Fabrics: An Illustrated Classification,* Washington D.C., The Textile Museum, 1966.

Girault, Louis. *Textiles Boliviens: Région de Charazani,* Catalogue du Musée de l'Homme, Series H: Amérique IV. Paris, Musée National d'Histoire Naturelle, 1969.

Goodell, Grace, "The Cloth of the Quechua," *Natural History.* New York, American Museum of Natural History, Dec. 1969.

Higgins, Kitty, and Kenny, David, *Bolivian Highland Weaving of the 18th, 19th and 20th Centuries.* Toronto, The Textile Museum, 1978.

Julien, Catherine J., *Inca Administration in the Titicaca Basin as Reflected at the Provincial Capital of Hatunquolla,* Ph.D. dissertation. Berkeley, University of California, 1975.

Kelemen, Pál, "The Weaver's High Art," *Americas.* Washington, D.C., Dept. of Cultural Affairs, Dec. 1966.

King, Mary Elizabeth, *Ancient Peruvian Textiles from the Collection of the Textile Museum, Washington, D.C.* New York, The Museum of Primitive Art, 1965.

Kubler, George, "The Quechua in the Colonial World," *Handbook of South American Indians,* Vol. 2; Bureau of American Ethnology Bulletin 143. Washington, D.C., Smithsonian, 1946.

LaBarre, Weston, "The Aymará Indians of the Lake Titicaca Plateau, Bolivia," *American Anthropologist,* Vol. 50, No. 1, Part 2, Memoir Series, No. 68. Menasha, Wisconsin, Jan. 1948.

Meisch, Lynn, *A Traveler's Guide to El Dorado and the Inca Empire.* New York, Simon and Schuster, 1977.

Mishkin, Bernard, "Contemporary Quechua," *Handbook of South American Indians,* Vol. 2; Bureau of American Ethnology Bulletin 143. Washington, D.C., Smithsonian, 1946.

Oblitas, Enrique, *Cultura Callawaya.* La Paz, Los Amigos del Libro, 1963.

Osborne, Harold, *Bolivia: Land Divided.* London and New York, Royal Institute of International Affairs; Oxford University Press, 1954–56.

––*Indians of the Andes: Aymarás and Quechuas,* Cambridge, Harvard University Press, 1952.

––*South American Mythology,* London/New York, Hamlyn Publishing Group, 1968.

Olen, Earl Leonard, *Bolivia: Land, People and Institutions.* Washington, D.C., Scarecrow Press, 1952.

Rigoberto Paredes, M., *Trajes y armas indígenas.* La Paz, Ediciones Isla, 1964, p. 22.

Rowe, Ann Pollard, *Warp-Patterned Weaves of the Andes,* Washington, D.C., The Textile Museum, 1977.

Ryden, Stig, *Archaeological Researches in the Highlands of Bolivia.* Göteborg, The Humanistic Fund of Sweden, 1947.

Tschopik, Harry, Jr., "The Aymará," *Handbook of South American Indians,* Vol. 2; Bureau of American Ethnology Bulletin 143. Washington, D.C., Smithsonian, 1946.

Wasserman, Emily (Tamara E.), *Gravestone Designs: Rubbings and Photographs from New York and New Jersey.* New York, Dover, 1972.

Weil, Thomas E., *Area Handbook for Bolivia.* Washington, D.C., n.d., [mid-1970s].

Fig. 1: *Lliclla,* mid-20th century, Kaalaya Village. 38½" x 42". Plain-weave stripes with double-cloth pattern bands; predominant color, maroon.

2

3

Department of La Paz: Charasani Valley

4

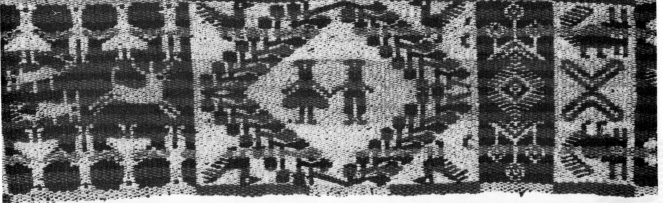

5

6

7

8

9

Fig. 2: Detail of *lliclla* in Fig. 1, featuring a horse, birds and an unusual representation of fish. **Fig. 3:** Detail of a *lliclla,* with birds, dogs, women in festival skirts and hats, and sun symbols (*inti*). **Figs. 4 & 5:** Hatbands, ca. 1975. Widths ½″ and 1″ (Coll. Tamara Wasserman). Finely woven with commercial trade threads. **Figs. 6–9:** Belts, mid-20th century (Coll. Tamara Wasserman). Double-faced weave with complementary warp sets. Typical geometrics with whimsical animals and people.

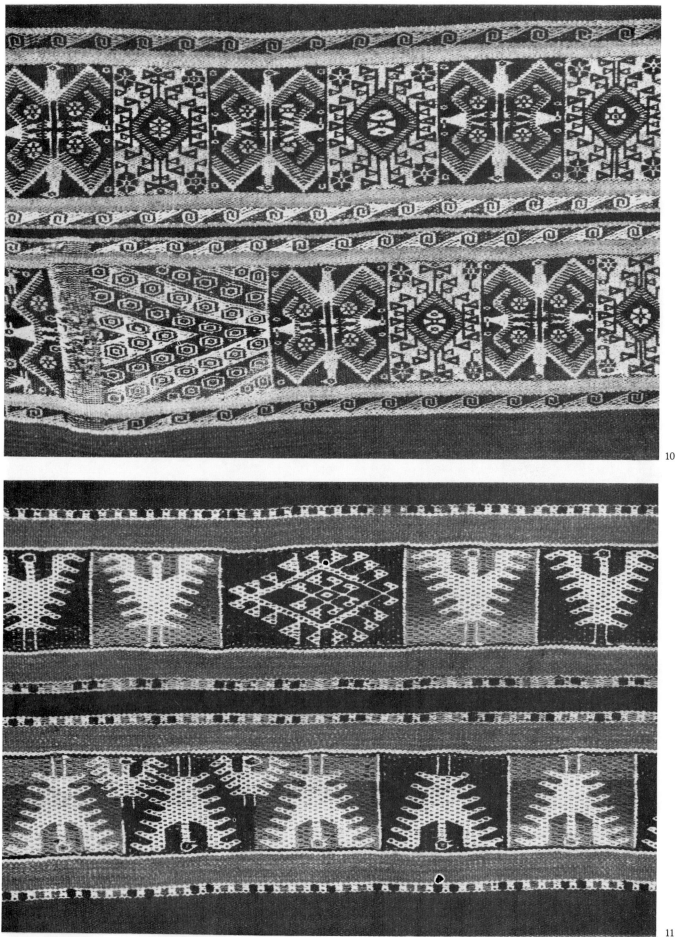

10

11

22   *Department of Potosí: Bolívar (top) and Pocoata (bottom)*

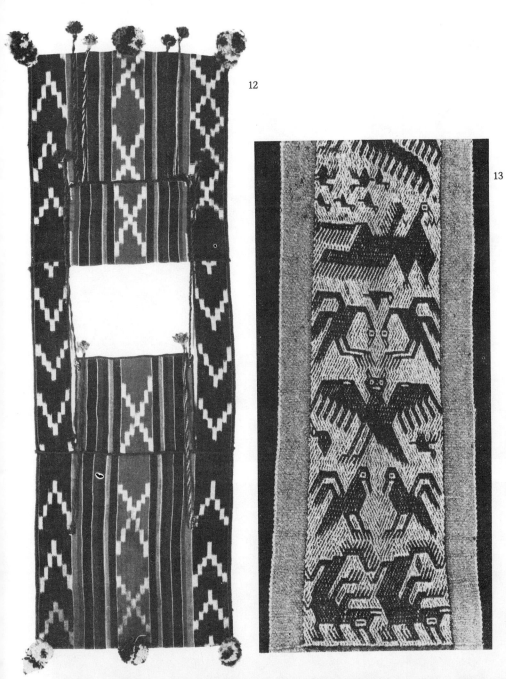

12

13

Details of central panels of *licllas,* mid-20th century. **Fig. 10:** 10″ x 20″. Paired condors and diamond motifs in brilliant colors. **Fig. 11:** 14″ x 28″. "Pebble-weave" patterning of identical birds in multihued segments. **Fig. 12:** Saddle-bag, mid-20th century, Tarabuco Region, possibly from Icla. 14″ x 40″. Unusual for its warp-*ikat* patterning. **Fig. 13:** Detail, 6″ x 18″, of *capote* (*poncho*), mid-20th century, Potolo Region. Pattern bands—in double-faced weave, using complementary warp sets—show owl (or bat) and paired birds. **Figs. 14 & 15:** Belts, mid-20th century. Widths 2½″ and 1½″. Double cloth with humorous zoomorphic figures.

14

15

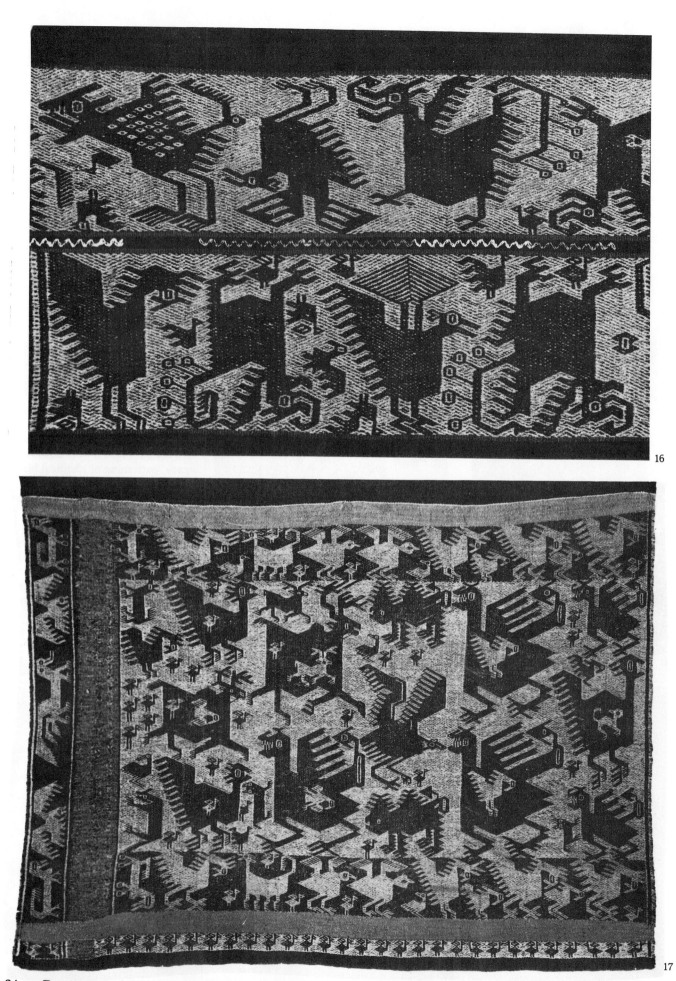

16

17

24   *Department of Potosí: Potolo Region*

18

Fig. 16: Detail, 8" x 16", of *lliclla*, mid-20th century. Fig. 17: Half-*aksu*, mid-20th century. 22½" x 28½" (Coll. Bob Koch). Both pieces are plain weave with pattern bands in double-faced weave using complementary warp sets. Outstanding examples of Potolan artistry. Various fantasy animals, including rare antlered deer. Fig. 18: Full *aksu*, mid-20th century. 28½" x 51½". Plain weave; design areas in double-faced weave using complementary warp sets. Fine, fully patterned *aksu* with saluting human figures set among lively birds, dogs and rabbits.

19

20

21

22

23

24

25

Figs. 19–23: *Sakas* (young girls' practice "samplers"), early to mid-20th century. Sizes from 3" to 12". **Fig 24:** Half-*aksu,* early 20th century. 22" x 23". Plain weave; pattern areas in double-faced weave using complementary warp sets. Fantastic "dragons" with looped tails and forked tongues. **Fig. 25:** *Chuspa,* mid-20th century, Tarabuco Region, Candelaria Village. 7" x 7". Black-and-white pouch used with the mourning costume (*luto*); compare Color Plate 25.

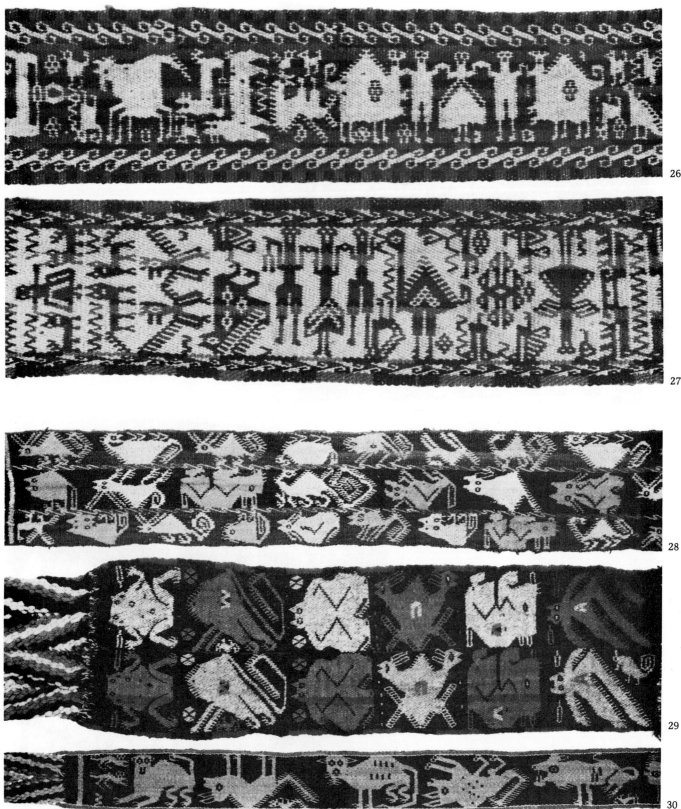

Figs. 26 & 27: Belts, mid-20th century. Widths 1½" and 2½". Double cloth. Imaginatively designed celebrants, joined by animals. **Figs. 28–30:** Belts, mid-20th century. Widths from 2" to 7". Double cloth. Lleque Village is known for such boldly drawn rodents, frogs and felines.

Departments of Cochabamba (top 2) and La Paz (bottom 3)

In these captions, warp count per inch and weft count per inch will be given as "W .../in." and "w .../in.," respectively. **Left:** Two women in their festival attire. The weaver, left, wearing a "rainbow-striped" *liclla*, carries her grandchild wrapped in a second weaving. Her daughter, right, wears two fine traditional *licllas*. **Below:** Detail, 14" x 16", of *liclla* seen above, early 20th century, Kanisaya Village. Full garment 43½" x 43½". W 108/in., w 20/in. Plain-weave stripes between pattern of double cloth with human, animal and geometric figures.

Left: Rare *liclla,* late 19th or early 20th century, Ulla Ulla Village. 35" x 40". W 96/in., w 26/in. Plain-weave stripes apparently of unplied and overspun imported merino wool; wide pattern bands of double-faced weave (with complementary warp sets) showing the *wajrapallay* motif; unusual chevron-patterned "painted-warp" *ikat* design bands. **Below:** Detail, 10" x 12", of *liclla* illustrated above. **Opposite, top:** Village women in festival dress. The woman at left wears a machine-made *manta* over her handwoven *liclla.* They all wear *winchas* under pressed-felt hats. **Opposite, bottom:** Classic *liclla,* early 20th century, Kaalaya Village. 33" x 43". W 60/in., w 20/in. Plain-weave stripes alternate with double-cloth pattern bands containing horses and the *wajrapallay* motif. The *ribete* is crossed-warp with diverted warps in *ojo de gato* pattern.

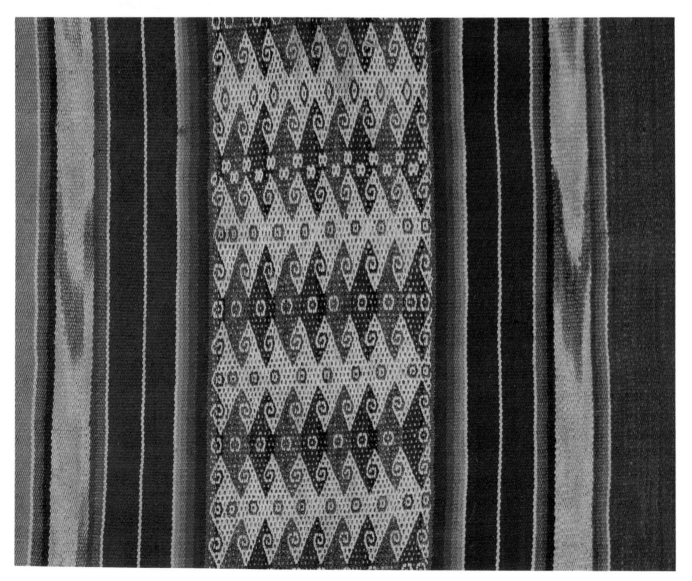

PLATE 2   *Department of La Paz: Charasani Valley*

Department of La Paz: Charasani Valley   PLATE 3

PLATE 4   *Department of La Paz: Charasani Valley*

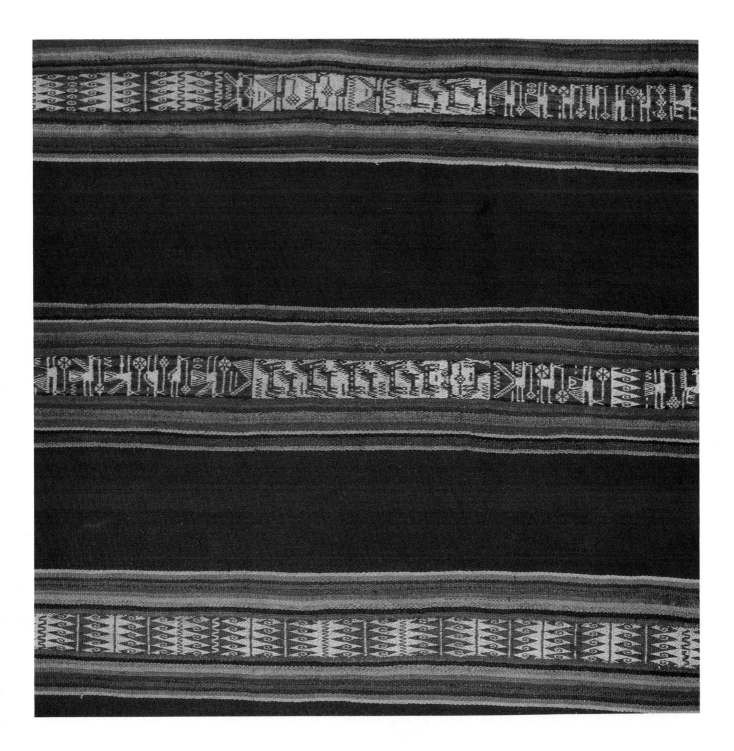

Opposite, top: *Winchas,* mid-20th century. Top to bottom, 2″ x 15½″ (Coll. Tamara Wasserman), 2″ x 18″, 2½″ x 20″. Double cloth, decorated with glass beads and coins. **Opposite, bottom:** *Capacho,* mid-20th century. 12″ x 14″. Plain-weave stripes alternate with double-cloth bands of *wajrapallay* and typical animals. **Above:** Detail of festival *poncho* worn by dignitaries and healers, early 20th century. Full garment 53″ x 54″. Plain-weave stripes between double-cloth pattern bands showing the *wajrapallay* motif and animals; separately woven fringe attached.

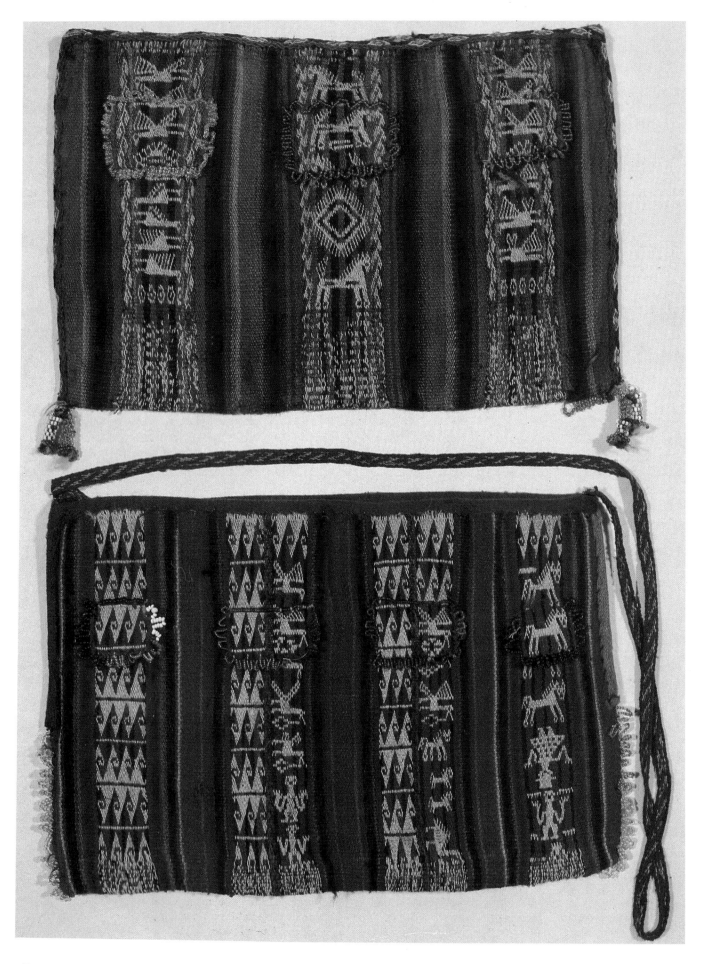

PLATE 6   *Department of La Paz: Charasani Valley*

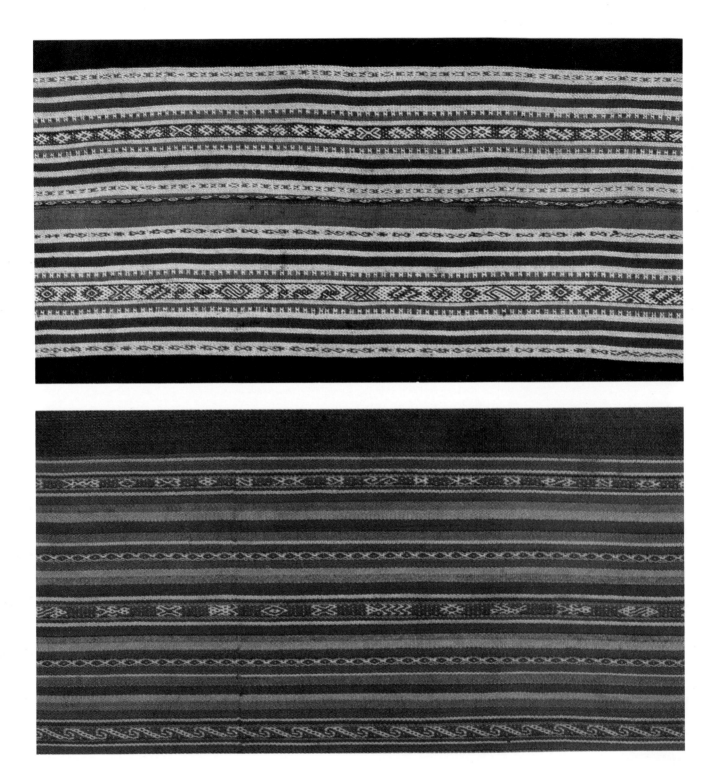

Opposite: *Chuspas* (*coca*-leaf pouches), mid-20th century. Top 7″ x 10½″, bottom 7″ x 10″. Plain weave with double-cloth pattern bands. The flap pockets — in which the lime catalyst, chewed with the leaves, is placed — are part of the continuous warp, woven on a special loom extension. **Above, top:** *Awayo*, late 19th or early 20th century. 35½″ x 41¾″. W 80/in., w 19/in. Plain weave with pattern bands of double-faced weave using complementary warp sets (the geometric and animal motifs are typical Aymará designs). **Above, bottom:** Detail, 12″ x 24″, of *awayo*, mid to late 19th century (Coll. Steve Berger). Full piece 21½″ x 37″. W 110/in., w 37/in. Same weave as the one above. May have been used as a ceremonial cloth for wrapping offerings.

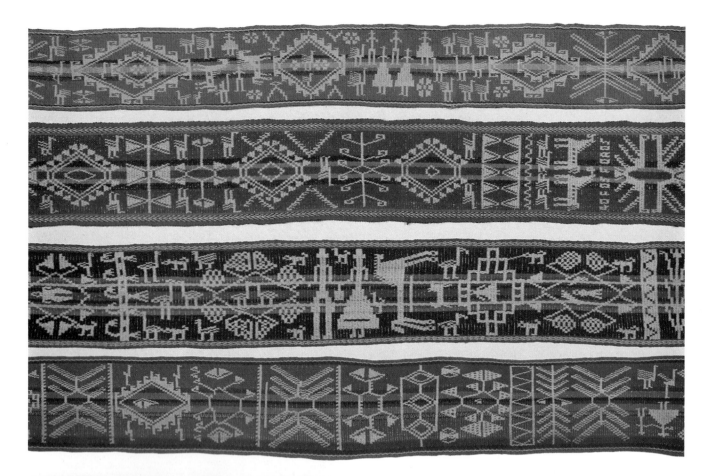

Above: Belts, early 20th century, Pacajes Province. Widths 2½" to 4". Double-faced weave using complementary warp sets. Geometric designs mingled with animal and human figures. The right end of the second belt is inscribed "40 fósforos" (40 matches). **Left:** Detail, 10" wide, of *poncho* from the Copacabana area, early to mid-20th century. Section of pattern band with frogs, birds, horsemen and sectored motifs. **Opposite, top:** *Balandrán poncho,* early 20th century, Aroma Province (Coll. Steve Berger). 65" x 73½". Plain weave with pattern bands (near center seam and along edges) in complementary warp weave. The narrow bands of wavy patterns are double-faced weave using complementary warp sets. Separately woven fringe attached. **Opposite, bottom:** Bag, late 19th or early 20th century. 12" x 14". Plain weave with pattern bands of double-faced weave using complementary warp sets. The "flowered lattice" pattern is probably based on Spanish Colonial influence.

PLATE 8   *Department of La Paz: Pacajes and Lake Titicaca Region*

PLATE 10 *Department of Potosí: Bolívar Region*

Opposite, top: Detail, 24" x 24", of matrimonial *aksu,* late 19th or early 20th century (Coll. Bob Koch). Full garment 44" x 52". Plain weave with pattern bands of double-faced weave using complementary warp sets. The detail features the band of "pebble-weave" birds. **Opposite, bottom:** Details of four *ribetes.* 8" long, showing a variety of patterned tubular edgings. **Right:** Matrimonial *aksu,* late 19th or early 20th century, Chalaviri Estancia (Coll. Bob Koch). 50" x 54". Plain weave, with geometric and scrolled pattern bands in double-faced weave using complementary warp sets, and double cloth. **Below:** Detail, 24" x 30", of the *aksu* above.

PLATE 12   *Department of Potosí: Bolívar Region*

Opposite, top: Matrimonial belt, late 19th or early 20th century. 2¾" x 78". Double-faced weave using complementary warp sets. At the upper end the warps are gathered into plaits; later the weaving resumes to end the belt. **Opposite, bottom:** Detail, 18" x 18", of an early and unusual matrimonial *aksu* containing "pebble-weave" pattern bands of stylized birds. **Above:** Detail, 12" x 12", of a rare ceremonial *poncho,* mid to late 19th century, Jorenko Estancia, Alawi Family (Coll. Steve Berger). Full garment 35" x 43". W 90/in., w 18/in. Plain weave with double-cloth pattern bands. The design represents a floral vine of the Andean highlands.

Chuspas, late 19th or early 20th century. 9″ x 10″ (left) and 8″ x 9″ (right). Plain weave, with pattern bands of double-faced weave using complementary warp sets, and double cloth. Tufted tassels at the bottom.

PLATE 14   *Department of Potosí: Bolívar Region*

Chuspas, mid-20th century. 6½" x 6½" (left) and 6" x 6" (right). Double cloth. Horseman, bird and diamond motifs; colorful wrapped tassels.

Top left: Detail, approx. width 12″, of *lliclla,* showing the S-shaped snake found also in ancient Peruvian textiles from the South Coast. **Top right:** Detail (16″ x 16″) of central band of *lliclla,* mid-20th century. Full garment 42½″ x 48″. W 60/in., w 30 in. Plain weave with double-cloth pattern band. Vibrant stripes, compressed by black alpaca background, create a multidimensional effect. **Bottom:** Detail, approx. width 12″, of central panel of *lliclla,* mid-20th century. Stylized condors and "sundiamond" patterns. **Opposite, top:** Belts, mid-20th century (Coll. Tamara Wasserman). Width 3″ x 4″, length 20″ to 28″. Double cloth. Like central bands of Bolívar *llicllas.* Condor designs. **Opposite, bottom:** Belts, mid-20th century (first and third, Coll. Tamara Wasserman). Width 4″ to 6″, length 25″ to 36″. Double cloth. "Snake and diamond" patterns.

PLATE 16   *Department of Potosí: Bolívar Region*

PLATE 18   *Department of Potosí: Town of Macha*

Opposite: Detail of *liclla,* mid-20th century. Full garment 43″ x 50″. W 80/in., w 19/in. Plain weave with pattern bands in double-faced weave using complementary warp sets. Central band has pattern of "eyes and zeros" bordered by small scroll motifs. **Above, top:** Detail of *liclla,* mid-20th century. Full garment 36½″ x 36½″. W 54/in., w 22/in. Plain weave with pattern areas in double-faced weave using complementary warp sets. "Pebble-weave" birds, animals, people—and even a truck. **Above, bottom:** Pattern band, 12″ x 36″, of *liclla,* mid-20th century (Coll. Tamara Wasserman). Plain-weave areas offset by intricate "twill"-patterned areas.

Above: Belts and *chuspa*, ca. 1970 (Coll. Tamara Wasserman). Width of belts 1¼"; *chuspa* 3½" x 3½". Supplementary-weft weave ("weft face") leaving no pattern on the reverse. **Left:** *Lliclla*, mid-20th century (Coll. Tamara Wasserman). 36" x 48". W 50/in., w 18/in. Plain weave with pattern bands in double-faced weave using complementary warp sets. Intricate lattice of sectored circles, trellises and stylized animals on 11 warp stripes. **Opposite, top:** *Bandera poncho* (also called *boliviano poncho*), mid-20th century (Coll. Tamara Wasserman). 24½" x 47½". W 96/in., w 20/in. Plain weave, with pattern bands in double-faced weave using complementary warp sets, and warp *ikat*. Separately woven fringe attached. **Opposite, bottom:** Detail, approx. width 30", of *bandera poncho*, early 20th century (Coll. Tamara Wasserman). Bottom edge features belt-like double-weave pattern band.

PLATE 20   *Department of Potosí: (bottom: Pocoata)*

Department of Potosí: Calcha Village   PLATE 21

PLATE 22 *Department of Potosí: Caiza Village (top) and Potolo Region (bottom)*

Opposite, top: *Poncho,* mid-20th century. 52½" x 57". W 54/in., w 16/in. Plain weave with evenly spaced warp-*ikat* bands containing step-pyramid designs. Separately woven, fringed band. **Opposite, bottom:** Half-*aksu,* mid-20th century. 24½" x 33½". W 64/in., w 20/in. Plain-weave stripes with pattern bands (dragon-like creature and stylized cats) in double-faced weave using complementary warp sets. Crossed-warp *ribete* with diverted warps in *ojo de gato* pattern. **Above:** *Capote* (festival *poncho*), early 20th century. 47" x 47½". W 70/in., w 21/in. Plain-weave stripes with pattern bands in double-faced weave using complementary warp sets. Design elements include four-winged birds, various animals and diamond-shaped mask motif similar to pre-Columbian stylized felines.

PLATE 24   *Department of Potosí: Potolo Region*

Opposite: Half-*aksu*, early 20th century. 24″ x 35″. W 88/in., w 22/in. Plain-weave stripes with pattern bands in double-faced weave using complementary warp sets. Crocheted *ribete*. Two large central bird-like creatures dominate the asymmetrical layout. Reportedly the antlered deer, also shown, once lived on the *altiplano*.

Above: *Chuspas*, early to mid-20th century, Candelaria and Presto Villages (upper and lower left, Coll. Tamara Wasserman). From 4″ x 4″ to 7″ x 7″. Plain weave with pattern areas in double-faced weave using complementary warp sets. Candelaria uses horses, llamas and people in the designs; Presto uses diamonds and zigzags.

PLATE 26   *Department of Chuquisaca: Tarabuco Region*

Opposite: Festival *unkus,* early to mid-20th century, Candelaria Village. 14″ x 19″ (top) and 19½″ x 21½″ (bottom). Double-faced weave using complementary warp sets. Separately woven fringe attached. Used as shoulder yokes or hip aprons. **Above:** Detail, 12″ x 12″, of the lower *unku* on the preceding page. Intricate figure work of horses, llamas and groups of people holding hands while walking in the fields or dancing.

PLATE 28   *Department of Chuquisaca: Tarabuco Region*

Opposite: Detail (approx. width 14″) of *aksu* (skirt), early 20th century. Candelaria Village. Design includes diamond-shaped *inti,* a Quechua sun symbol. **Above, top:** *Aksu,* early 20th century, Candelaria Village. 29″ x 41½″. W 52/in., w 15/in. Plain weave with pattern bands of double-faced weave using complementary warp sets. The horses in the design are vestiges of Spanish influence. **Above, bottom:** *Poncho,* mid-20th century. 30½″ x 54″. W 80/in., w 18/in. Plain weave. Separately woven fringe attached, reminiscent of Inca featherwork. Embroidered diamond stitch decorates seam between the two pieces.

PLATE 30   *Department of Potosí*

Opposite, top: Details of belts, ca. 1960–70 (Coll. Tamara Wasserman). Width 1″ to 2½″. Double-faced weave using complementary warp sets, and double cloth. Designs include kissing birds; buses, fish and mice (on the one inscribed "Adela Arena"); stylized horses; and perhaps a helicopter. **Opposite, bottom:** Details of belts, ca. 1960–70 (middle three, Coll. Tamara Wasserman). Width 1″ x 2½″. Same weaves as above. Designs include guitars, birds, field mice and other animals.

Above, top: Details of belts, mid-20th century, Huancarani and Sanipaya Villages. Width 1½″ to 2½″. Double cloth. Bizarre human and animal caricatures. Lowest one inscribed "Damián Torrico." **Above, bottom:** Detail of belt, early to mid-20th century. Full belt 7½″ x 40″. Woven in three separate pieces and sewn together. Includes 67 figures of birds, domestic animals and horsemen.

W. Area of Department of Cochabamba (top); Unknown Area (bottom)   PLATE 31

Top: Detail of festival sash, mid-20th century. Full sash 6¼" x 55". Double-faced weave using complementary warp sets. Human and animal figures. **Center:** Details of belts, ca. 1960–70 (third, Coll. Tamara Wasserman).

Width 1" to 2½". Double cloth. **Bottom:** Detail, 4" x 16", of belt, mid 20th-century (Coll. Tamara Wasserman). Double cloth. 77 horses with mounted and unmounted riders.

PLATE 32   *La Paz: Ayata (top); Potosí (center and bottom)*